craft
  for a
     Dry Lake

Kim Mahood

Doubleday

Where I have thought it advisable or might cause embarrassment
I have altered the names of people mentioned in the text.

CRAFT FOR A DRY LAKE
A DOUBLEDAY BOOK

First published in Australia and New Zealand in 2000
by Anchor

Copyright © Kim Mahood, 2000

All rights reserved. No part of this publication may be reproduced,
stored in a retrieval system, transmitted in any form or by any means,
electronic, mechanical, photocopying, recording or otherwise, without
the prior written permission of the publisher.

National Library of Australia
Cataloguing-in-Publication Entry

   Mahood, Kim.
   Craft for a dry lake.

   ISBN 1 86359 139 7.

   1. Mahood, Kim – Childhood and youth. 2. Artists, Australian – Journeys.
   3. Alice Springs (N.T.) – Biography. I. Title

920.72

Transworld Publishers,
a division of Random House Australia Pty Ltd
Level 3, 100 Pacific Highway, North Sydney, NSW 2060

Random House New Zealand Limited
18 Poland Road, Glenfield, Auckland

Transworld Publishers (UK) Limited
61–63 Uxbridge Road, Ealing, London W5 5SA

Random House Inc
1540 Broadway, New York, New York 10036

Edited by Julia Stiles
Cover and text design by Gayna Murphy, Greendot Design
Cover photograph courtesy of Pamela Lofts
Typeset in 11.5/14pt Bembo by Midland Typesetters, Maryborough, Victoria
Printed and bound by Griffin Press

*To my father,
whose death made the book necessary.*

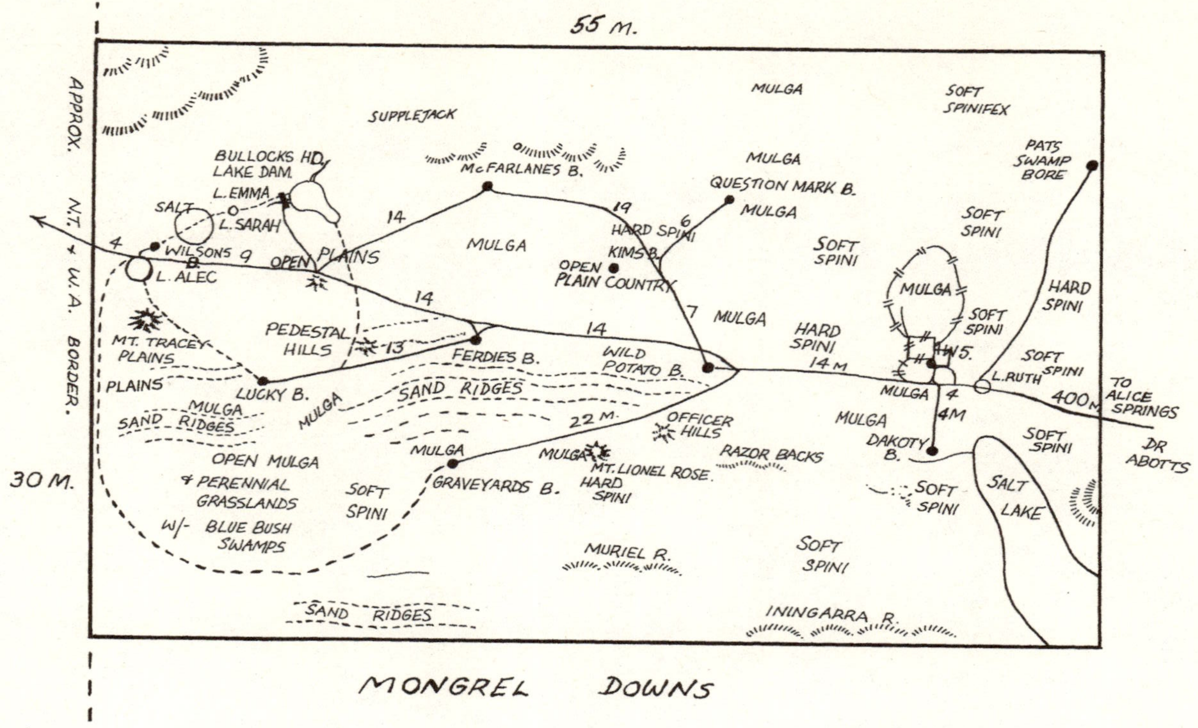
55 M.
30 M.
APPROX. N.T. + W.A. BORDER.
MONGREL DOWNS
SUPPLEJACK
MULGA
SOFT SPINIFEX
PATS SWAMP BORE
BULLOCKS HD. LAKE DAM.
L. EMMA
SALT
L. SARAH
McFARLANES B.
QUESTION MARK B.
WILSONS B.
L. ALEC
OPEN PLAINS
HARD SPINI
KIMS B.
OPEN PLAIN COUNTRY
SOFT SPINI
PEDESTAL HILLS
MT. TRACEY PLAINS
PLAINS
FERDIES B.
WILD POTATO B.
LUCKY B.
SAND RIDGES
OFFICER HILLS
RAZOR BACKS
MT. LIONEL ROSE.
GRAVEYARDS B.
OPEN MULGA
+ PERENNIAL GRASSLANDS
W/- BLUE BUSH SWAMPS
MURIEL R.
ININGARRA R.
L. RUTH
DAKOTY B.
SALT LAKE
TO ALICE SPRINGS
400 M
DR ABOTTS
14 M
22 M.
4M

*This was my father's country, or so I thought
returning on some half-cocked pilgrimage
to lay old ghosts, eschew old myths,
or some such middle-life conceit.
And found country, dry, a dry place
that resisted memory,
cattle trodden, beer cans and dead cars along the track,
a route much favoured by blackfellows on grog runs to Rabbit
Flat.
Found country that could not hold the past,
that was another place.*

*The black women gave me my old skin back
and made it new,
but I could not wear it.
The dreaming tracks are not mine.*

*I left relieved, believing
this place held nothing for me,
a chapter closed.
And leaving, felt an old wound seep,
draining griefs too deep
to be mine alone.
Felt something reach.
An old, hard grip, subtle as blood
closing about the bone.*

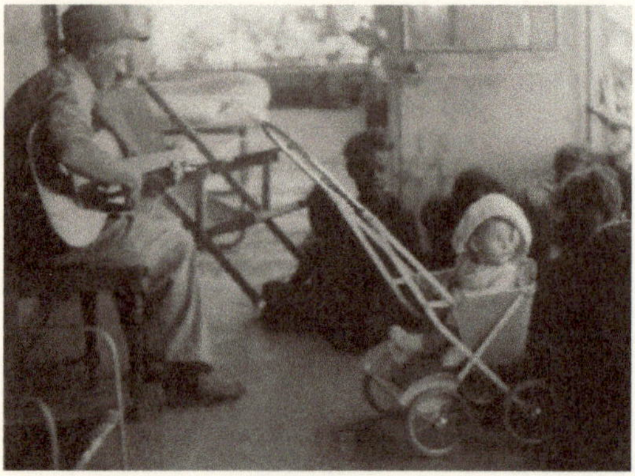

1

WE HAD ALWAYS BEEN CLOSE. He took me with him sometimes on short trips when I was very small, driving along the railway line from Finke because it afforded a better, though bumpier, route than the sandy track through the dunes. I divined my specialness to him early, and it was precious to me. When the drinking began to affect his moods I still felt the specialness, but with it a responsibility to something dark and sad that surfaced in him.

He drove slowly, his elbows on the steering wheel when he wanted to roll a cigarette. I learned to roll them for him because when he did it he would also be looking out of the window at the country, or cattle, or looking for tracks. He never actually ran into anything, but sometimes it was pretty close. We began then the long conversation which was to continue between us until his death.

He told me about being a small boy on the outskirts of Sydney during the Depression years. He would take a spud and a billycan and paddle down the river, happy to be by himself, dreaming of the day when he would go bush. There was a strange, heavy young woman who lived alone in a shack near the river. She made an impression on him because of her solitariness, and because she clearly did not belong with those women who became mothers and wives and sisters. He helped her with her horse, riding it and feeding it when she went away. His name was Alec then, short for Alexander, but his brother had already given him the nickname that would stick to him in its truncated version for the rest of his life. Joe Blow the Bushie.

He told me about the milk run he did when he was ten, seven days a week for a shilling a day, getting up at four a.m. to do four hours work before school. He told of the places where he delivered the milk, the old horse which pulled the milk cart stopping of its own accord at each house. There was the grand house on the hill, which had once been a squatter's residence, and a kind, quiet woman who gave him a book. There was the house where the fleas jumped into his socks before he got to the door, and when the door opened the stink nearly made him retch. Each week the milkman would count out my father's pay, day by day, reluctantly—Monday, I think you worked on Monday. What about Tuesday? Were you here on Tuesday?

My father never missed a day, every shilling counting towards the family's survival. Grudgingly the milkman would hand over the seven shillings. My father always chuckled, recounting the story. Every week the milkman tempted himself to cheat the ten-year-old boy, and every week he could not quite manage to do it.

He told me about the lay preacher who was an ex-burglar. The local church was a little solitary building in a clearing in the bush. The burglar would peddle up on his bicycle in the evening with his whizzbang box of tricks and deliver his sermon accompanied by flashes of electricity to signify lightning bolts from God. After the service he would peddle off into the darkness with his toolbox of batteries and screwdrivers, and my father could not help wondering whether the burglar was a truly reformed character or whether the toolbox served a dual purpose. It was about this time that he ceased to believe in the Sunday school God and began to find his own sense of life in the bush which still spread fingers along the river and into the edges of the city.

During the Depression his father had occasional relief work, and his mother grew forbidden rhubarb in wooden boxes under the house. They lived on the outskirts of Sydney, seven of them in a tiny ramshackle Depression house on which his father did running repairs to keep it habitable. When the kitchen floor rotted out, his father co-opted him and his mother to help steal a wooden tent floor from the nearby army base. After dark, on a weekend when the army was out on manoeuvres, the three of them slipped among the canvas-lined streets to the tent his father had selected. His mother wore a cap and was disguised as a man.

His father said—If we meet anyone, I'll do the talking.

Between them they lifted the wooden platform intact and stole away unchallenged. By daylight the tent floor had been transformed into a new kitchen floor.

My father watched his intelligent, angry father flirt with the Communist Party. His father had the eccentric and strongly-held views of the self-educated, and a grievance. At the age of four he had been placed in an orphanage, although his parents were both still living. Conditions in the orphanage amounted to child slave labour, and at fourteen he ran away and joined the navy. For most of his life he believed he was illegitimate, since a younger sibling had been kept at home. It was not until he saw his birth certificate, when he was an old man, that he knew for certain this was not the case.

One of my father's early recollections was of being taken

by his father to his grandmother's deathbed. The two small boys, my father and his older brother, were sent in to see the dying old lady, whom they had never seen before, and who presumably had never seen them. Her angry, unforgiving son stayed outside. There was no deathbed reconciliation, and I suppose she died grieving for the son she had left to fate.

His services to the Party consisted mainly of pasting up posters after dark and occasionally providing a meeting room. Small groups of men and women came to the house, women such as my father had never seen, opinionated intellectuals who smoked and held their own with the men. His own shy gentle mother served them cups of tea and stayed quietly in the background. It seemed to him that these sophisticated aliens exploited his father, giving him menial dangerous chores and excluding him from serious intellectual discussion. The liaison broke down abruptly when a Party speaker at a rally took exception to some of my grandfather's questions and accused him of never having had it tough. He attacked the orator with a shovel and had to be pulled off.

My father went sometimes to stay with friends of the family who lived in a cottage on the North Shore. Their house was full of books and music and pleasant conversation, and he found a haven in the unostentatious expression of culture which did not exist in his own home. He would wander about the streets of the leafy suburb, gazing through ironwork gates at the imposing mansions in their islanded calm of flowerbeds and trees. He neither resented nor aspired to the wealth he saw, but he knew with a certainty beyond resolve that he would leave his parents' world and follow the dream that had begun during his solitary journeys on the river.

There is a school photograph of my father taken at around this time, sitting among about thirty other children, his classmates at the Western Sydney high school he attended. You don't see children who look like that in Australia any more. They were drawn from an area hard hit by the Depression, most families including my father's were on the dole. Many of the children are barefoot. The clothes are ragged, too large or too small. Faces show the marks of poor diet and congenital illnesses. My father's face, with its jutting ears and bright smile, is one of the few that shines out with a clear hopeful intelligence.

My father does not seem to have stepped into his real life until he left his family and childhood behind. When I examine the early stories more closely, they are full of waiting, of dreaming. His father looms large, too preoccupied with his own outrage and the vicissitudes of poverty to offer his family much in the way of affection. Younger siblings, a baby brother born with brain damage, absorb most of his mother's energy. On his first day of high school he discovers that he has his older brother's larrikin reputation to live down. The headmaster, hearing the name Mahood, says aghast—my God, not another one.

The headmaster's fears are unfounded. My father is shy, hard-working and intelligent. He is also somewhere else for much of the time. He rides the bus home after school, so absorbed in reverie that he travels miles beyond his stop. On the return journey he drifts back into daydream, and misses his stop again. His older brother, who has been sent to meet the bus, watches in disbelief as it sails past carrying his brother with it. Around the boy my father the Depression years are overtaken by the War years. In his third year of high school the students are given vocational guidance tests. The brightest boys among them, my father included, are advised to become fitters and turners, to be trained in the manufacture of delicate components for arms technology. No suggestion of finishing secondary school, of higher education, of a life after the war. This piece of cynicism makes a lasting impression on my father. He draws, he learns to play the guitar, and quietly withdraws from the family aspirations for him to acquire a trade, to get a job and to make a safe and unremarkable life for himself.

His older brother, who has joined the navy with great enthusiasm, comes home on his first leave and tears down all the patriotic posters he has taped to the walls of their shared bedroom. The larrikin sailor and clown lies morosely on his bed and refuses to talk. My father takes a job in a dairy. He is fifteen.

The mud and milk and cowshit of the dairy, the days regimented to the rhythms of cows' udders, are not his idea of escape. He throws in the job and goes north.

From this moment of departure there is a shift in the tempo of the stories. The shy daydreamer retreats and a young man full of vitality takes his place. He has come out into air he can breathe, and relishes it. Cutting cane, jumping trains, being threatened with arrest for vagrancy, he is on the road to his own future.

His first job as a stockman was among the stony ridges and gullies north of Mt Isa, working for a family who had a little property several days ride from the Dobbyn, not far from the Gunpowder River. It was packhorse access only, and the campsites were platforms built in trees, with flour, tea and sugar stored out of reach of floods and predators. The men were constantly on the move, track-riding their own cattle, looking for the tracks of strange cattle, making sorties through the rocky gullies of no-man's-land. The largest property in the area, owned by a company, was considered fair game. The battlers' blocks which surrounded it fed like ticks on a fat cow, stealing unbranded stock at every opportunity, building their herds by the grace of the absentee landowner. But the stockmen employed by the company were smart men, and plenty of them had worked at one time or another on the other side of the boundary, and knew all the tricks. My father learned to wipe out tracks with a bush, to break up and scatter the charred sticks from the tiny campfires used to boil the billy. He learned the routes along stony creek beds which slowed wild cattle and showed no tracks. He learned to ride lookout, high along the crests of the hills, and to give the soft hooting cry of warning which carries so far and belongs in kind to the sounds of the bush.

To a young man of seventeen it was the best life imaginable. Among these half-wild, semiliterate men he discovered a code of behaviour which suited something quietly anarchic in his nature. They lived like bushrangers, stealing from the wealthy company landowners, but treating other battlers with scrupulous fairness. They valued practical skill and native intelligence, had a knowledge of the country so deeply ingrained it was like an intuition, were capable of extravagant acts of physical courage. Uncompromising virtues, uncontaminated with self-reflection. You measured up, or you didn't. I met one of these characters years later, after my father's death, an old reptile who looked me over leeringly in the presence of his wife, and asked me if I was single. He also said—He was a smart man, your dad. But drink. He could really put it away.

My father worked briefly for Mt Isa Mines, around the time of the big strike. His job was to watch the conveyor belt which carried the ore, breaking up the larger chunks as they went past. He used to act it out for us, poised and twitching, an imaginary sledgehammer raised, eyes fixed on an approaching lump of ore. As it got nearer he would tense, make several false starts with the hammer, swing wildly and miss, then pursue the fast-moving rock, taking hapless swipes until it disappeared. He said that gloves and pickaxes frequently came travelling along the conveyor belt, and he was always anticipating the appearance of an arm or a leg.

He didn't last long at the job, in spite of the money. Crossing the border into the Territory, he went back to cattle and horses, working his way across the Barkly Tablelands and eventually taking a job on Victoria River Downs. The immense pastoral holding was part of the Bovril empire, owned by an English lord and run along the lines of the English feudal system. It ran several stock camps almost continuously, and in spite of the exploitative conditions attracted top stockmen from all over the north. Most of them were less interested in the money than in the lifestyle, and in measuring themselves against their peers. Stock work required horsemanship and endurance, skill, quick reflexes and physical courage. To be a good stockman meant belonging to an elite. A photograph taken at the time shows my father on horseback, wearing a bandolier of bullets and with a rifle over his shoulder. Scrub bulls made the huge scattered herds difficult to control, and were chased and executed in the course of the work.

Owing to the size of the operation, working at Victoria River Downs also provided one of the few opportunities to meet young women, several of whom were employed in various capacities by the station. My mother, travelling on a collision course with my father, arrived from the Kimberleys and was employed in the store.

MY PARENTS WERE BOTH TALKERS. I know their stories almost as well as I know my own. They came north, my mother from Perth and my father from Sydney, each compelled by a dream of escape, adventure and opportunity. My mother, with a university degree and the beginnings of a career in journalism, was in search of adventure, leaving behind her the conventions and social constraints of the city. In her energetic pursuit of 'copy' among the eccentrics and individualists of the Outback, she transformed herself into one of them. She discovered on her return to the city that she could no longer curb and curtail herself to the requirements of city life.

My father was driven by a dream fuelled by a love of solitude, and the need to escape the poverty and limitations of Sydney. He knew when he left that he would never return.

And so my parents converged from the western and eastern edges of the continent. They were both fleeing something they had experienced as narrow-minded and restrictive, the creeping conservatism which had settled over the Australian psyche. It was the late 1940s, and they travelled towards a place which had existed powerfully in the imaginations of both long before they set out on their journeys towards it. What they found when they arrived was a kind of frontier, a tremendous and dramatic stage with a handful of players, and the opportunity for everyone to have a starring role, to write the drama as they went along.

There is a fine, fearless quality about my young parents. When they married, my mother owned a motor bike and a camera, my father a swag and a guitar. They had attempted, on the plea of my mother's family, to save two hundred pounds before they married. My father took a job with the stock and station firm of Wesfarmers in Perth, while my mother worked as a journalist with *Hoofs and Horns* in Adelaide. In my mother's absence a doctor's daughter in Perth made a play for the handsome young ex-ringer, inviting him to concerts and dinners, introducing him to the local social set. My father innocently accepted the invitations and told my mother about them in his regular letters. Deducing the intentions of the doctor's daughter, my mother sent the engagement ring back. She also threw in her job and caught the train to Alice Springs.

Wesfarmers reluctantly gave my father two weeks' leave when he threatened to resign. He flew to Adelaide, discovered my mother had already decamped, and flew to Alice Springs, where he met the train. My mother was resolute in her refusal to listen to his explanations. She hitchhiked north. My father followed. Sometimes they caught lifts on the same truck. In Katherine, his two weeks' leave expired, my father sent a telegram to Wesfarmers saying—Back next Monday. My mother went west to Humbert River to visit her sister, who was working as a governess. My father went too. He sent his employers another telegram—Back next Monday. When the Humbert River residents travelled to Katherine for the races, my parents went with them. In Katherine my father, carrying the stuffed crocodile he had bought as a gift for his future mother-in-law, hailed the local taxi driver. He explained to my mother that if she would not marry him here, immediately, he and the crocodile would take the taxi to Darwin and she would never see him again. My mother, with the encouragement of most of Katherine's population, said yes. A white dress, several sizes too large, was located in a hawker's van and altered to fit. A wedding ring was loaned for the occasion. My father's hair was trimmed, and white shirt and trousers bought at the store. The Salvation Army padre performed the second marriage ceremony to take place in Katherine and a grader driver took the wedding photographs. A slightly flustered congratulatory telegram arrived from my grandmother in Perth, addressed to Marie and Joe, Northern Territory. My father sent Wesfarmers another telegram saying—Back next Monday.

It was fortunate, after five weeks absence, that my father

still had his job, since the combined finances of my parents when they arrived in Perth was twelve pounds, ten of which were owed in back rent. But the job was merely an interim. My parents were Territorians. Shortly before I was born my father took a position as acting superintendent on the recently established Aboriginal settlement of Hooker Creek, seven hundred miles south-west of Darwin. When my mother attempted to send a telegram from the local post office to tell my father of my arrival, she was informed that there was no such place. A few weeks later she set out, baby in tow, for the nonexistent place, five hundred dirt track miles from the nearest town of Katherine.

My mother has written of these early years when my father was employed by the Department of Native Affairs. It was the fifties, an era of government rationing and the policy of assimilation for Aborigines. It was also an era of entrenched bureaucratic inefficiency. In the first months of my father's employment, the settlement was left without rations for the Aborigines, who fortunately were traditional Warlpiri people only recently in from the bush, still efficient hunters and gatherers. There was no kerosene to run lights and refrigerators, medical supplies consisted of aspirin and sulphur tablets, and for much of the time there was no vehicle. The vehicle, apart from providing transport, was also needed to maintain the bore, the settlement's only water supply, and to recharge the battery for the radio, the only means of communication. During this time my father became seriously ill with malaria, and several Aborigines died of it. My mother, without medical training or quinine, dosed and cared for her sick husband and half the population of the camp.

It is difficult these days to imagine an Aboriginal community (not to mention a young couple with a small baby) being abandoned for months without food, medical supplies, electricity, refrigeration, transport, radio contact and potentially without water. My father's brief, under these conditions, was to build housing for the people, break in horses and train stockmen in order to establish a cattle operation, carry out medical services and do the necessary administration and paperwork involved in running a community. All this he did, and worried that it was his own inadequacy that made the job so difficult. He wired up torch batteries to run the radio, planted a vegetable garden, took horses to the cattle station of Wave Hill to borrow flour, stitched wounds and splinted broken limbs after the frequent battles of the volatile Warlpiri. His suggestion that the type of housing he was expected to build was not appropriate for traditional Aboriginal people was ignored. So was his suggestion that standardised spelling of Aboriginal names would eliminate the confusion as to how many individuals actually lived on the community.

In spite of the frustrations, my parents were very happy on Hooker Creek, but my father had established himself as an upstart. After a year he was summarily banished to a mosquito-ridden mangrove swamp on the coast west of Darwin. My health deteriorated, and my parents were relocated to Beswick in Arnhem Land, where my father had the position of deputy superintendent. But his days with Native Affairs were numbered. Promotion was out of the question, and he did not have the temperament for compromise. In Central Australia a legendary character known as Colonel Rose ran a hand-picked team of stock inspectors who were working on eradicating pleuropneumonia and tuberculosis from the cattle population of the region. Although it was a government operation, Colonel Rose was notorious for hurling paperwork and official directives into the wastepaper basket and insisting that his stock inspectors be left in peace to do their jobs. He was outrageous, authoritarian and highly respected.

In later years he owned a pet eagle and a three-legged retriever, careering about town with both creatures in a Mini-Moke. When he was apprehended for dangerous driving, it transpired that he had not held a driving licence for years.

After the self-serving inefficient bureaucratic pettiness of the Department of Native Affairs, this was the kind of man for whom my father wanted to work. On learning that my father was employed by Native Affairs, the Colonel snorted in disgust and turned him down out of hand. But he made inquiries, discovered my father was in disgrace with the department, and relented.

My memories begin soon after this. My father was allocated the southern region of Central Australia as his jurisdiction, with the tiny railway town of Finke as his base. It is at Finke that my own sense of country has its beginnings, on the bank of the wide dry ancient pink river which cuts its way through the sandstone cliffs and red dunes of the Simpson Desert. It was during these years that the Centre succumbed to a drought so relentless that the wild camels died in their hundreds on the edge of stinking pools of mud, and one summer it was so hot that birds died in midflight and fell from the sky like feathered stones. On a trip to Adelaide my mother had to explain to me that the strange green stuff in front of the houses was grass. Finke exists even now in my memory with a hallucinatory clarity, its dust storms and the relentless three hundred and sixty degrees of horizon. Like calves born in times of drought, I did not know anything else, and cherished it.

Finke briefly gained notoriety after a fancy-dress party in

which my parents participated. For some reason it is always thought a good joke for men to dress as women, and the women played their less adventurous part and dressed as men. A band of fettlers from down the line got drunk at the pub and crashed the party, picking a fight with the first man they encountered. He shrieked and bolted, and the fearsome hairy-armed women of Finke removed their high-heeled shoes and waded into the fray. It took a while for the rumour of a band of Simpson Desert Amazons to die down, and Finke chuckled into its beer for months afterwards.

After four years at Finke we relocated to Alice Springs. By this time I had a brother and a very new sister. The years spent in Alice provided a hiatus in the adventurous trajectory of my parents' lives. It was a domestic period of small children, pony clubs, schools and neighbours. My mother taught French at the local high school, and my father continued to work as a stock inspector, spending much of his time out bush. He brought it back with him on his return, in his dust-covered Land Rover and battered felt hat.

And then there is the story that took a grip on my father's life and the life of my family, that continues to retell itself through my own life, full of loose ends and unfinished business.

2

My father's work took him all over the southern part of the Territory, and he would take his sketchbook and camp alone in the bush, making watercolour sketches and notes. After his death, among his trunkful of papers, I found the sketchbooks, notations in line and colour of his twin passions for painting and for the empty arid landscapes of the Centre. They record places which these days are tourist glamour spots—Chambers Pillar, Gosse Bluff—easily accessible by four-wheel drive and well-maintained roads. In my father's time access was via sandy and treacherous station tracks, if there were tracks at all.

A couple of years after the move to Alice my father decided to resign from his job as a stock inspector and work full-time as an artist. He was a very good cartoonist and had a number of commercial options to take up. Alice Springs was expanding fast as a tourist centre, with a growing market for local artists. When his friends heard about his intention to leave his job for the sake of his art, the rumour swept Alice Springs. Have you heard about Joe, poor bugger? He's quitting his job because of his 'eart.

Shortly before he tendered his resignation, the opportunity arose to be part of a land party which would set out from Alice Springs to search for a stock route from the southern Kimberleys to Central Australia. The Centre was recovering from years of drought. Cattle numbers were severely depleted, and disease-free breeding cows were available in the Kimberleys. The feasibility of the route had long been considered, and the time seemed right to make an attempt at it. In February of 1962 good rains had fallen, and the possibility was raised of bringing cattle overland on surface waters.

My father was thirty-four. He had a wife, four children and a drinking problem. He was never happier than when he was alone in the bush. The chance of making a trip into unknown country was irresistible.

In April of 1962 the six-man party set out on a due west compass bearing from the abandoned mine site of the Granites to the Aboriginal mission of Balgo in Western Australia. Although much of the country was wet and boggy, the direct route did not find usable stock water, and at Balgo a light plane was chartered to fly back over the route. Several large claypans which appeared to be fresh water were located to the south of the original traverse. The plane returned to Balgo and three of the party flew back to Alice Springs, leaving my father, Bill Wilson and Milton Willick to make the more circuitous return journey with the vehicles. Bill and Milton were both excellent bushmen, and for my father this part of the trip was pure pleasure. His expedition report is published in the July 1962 edition of a small journal called *Australian Territories*.

The country improved as we travelled east the following day and 17 miles from Mt Phyllis we found a lush Bluebush swamp—every type of feed imaginable—with water suitable for horses. We knew we were close to a large redwater claypan and, only a couple of miles further on, we drove straight onto it . . .

Our next find was a big white claypan (also containing usable water) which was marked on our map. Because of its shape we called it Bullock's Head Lake. This was good country with ironstone gravel flats covered in many good grasses and top feed . . . It was important now to find another water source within 30 or 40 miles of the red claypan. The next couple of days tested all our abilities to read the signs for finding large quantities of water. A symbolic plaque or painting for the entire trip would show a man on the roof of his vehicle, in a sea of spinifex, trying to penetrate the distance with binoculars. We spent a full day following birds and country contours to water, where, in Bill's words, 'If you camped on it for three days with a galah and a mouse, you'd have to give them a dry day.'

Two days later we had largely mapped this area by taking frequent bearings on 'willy-willys' off Bullock's Head Lake. It was 54 miles from the red claypan before we found an excellent waterhole with a hard-packed sandy edge and bottom, hidden among dense tea-tree and huge anthills. We named it Lake Ruth. This lake was about 40 miles west of The Granites, so we knew then that the cattle would make it.

All this is history. After a couple of days in Alice Springs, Bill Wilson went back and dragged a heavy chain along the route we had followed to give the cattle a track to follow. He met the overland cattle at Mt Phyllis, and delivered them, 1008 cows strong, to Milton and Bill Waudby at the Granites.

There is nothing in the clear, well-written account to indicate where this journey would take my father, but I remember the spaces that opened up in his voice when he spoke about it. When the idea of applying for a pastoral lease in the Tanami was raised, it did not take him long to make his choice between art and country.

3

MY MOTHER IS STILL A TALKER. She is a popular public speaker, a chewer on ears, a deliverer of soap-box harangues at the smallest provocation. She talks, when no-one else is available, to the radio, the bettongs which she feeds on the back lawn, the cat, the magpies, herself. She provides a running commentary on what she is doing, should be doing, will be doing. She does this whether anyone is listening or not. Her talk overflows into the written word. It is often designed to provoke a reaction. It is rich with contradiction, opinion and recollection. She has the stamina of the true talker and has won many arguments simply on the basis of her ability to talk longer than anyone else.

My mother always believed herself to be plain. In the folklore of her childhood she was the clever one, her blonde sister the pretty one. In fact many women have made themselves into beauties with fewer natural assets than my mother. As a young woman she had dark reddish-brown hair, beautiful green eyes, good cheekbones and a wide mouth which smiled readily. She had a small neat athletic body, which maintained itself, in spite of heavy smoking and the birth of four children, well beyond middle age.

My mother is not introspective. She was not introspective as a child and she has never been an introspective adult. She is optimistic, opinionated, contradictory, infuriating, courageous and rarely indulges in self-pity. The picture I have of her as a child is not much different. On winter nights in Alice Springs when my father was away on a bush trip she would tell stories of her childhood. They differ from my father's stories because, although the rather brash tomboy who was my mother is at the centre of the stories, they are in some essential sense not about her.

They are peopled with a compelling and eccentric cast of characters, they are rich with drama and humour. There is her domineering grandmother (who my mother resembles in appearance), who was rigidly opinionated, loathed men, Catholics and the Irish, in that order, and ruled the lives of her children until she died. There is her gentle and long-suffering grandfather, a surrogate father figure, who was a builder, and who put the garden hose through the bedroom window when Grandma had taken to her bed and was moaning for water. There is Connie, my mother's mother, who married a Scotsman and had two daughters, divorced him at the instigation of her mother, and ran a boarding house instead. There is my mother's younger sister, Yellin' Helen. There are the neighbours, 'Ector and Harthur Giles, Harthur being responsible for the unforgettable description of a local storekeeper—Missus, 'e's so tight you couldn't ram a pin hup 'is harse.

My mother's story is set during the Depression in a small West Australian country town and moves between York and Perth, as Grandma leaves to become a businesswoman and property owner in Victoria Park, and then returns when she hears rumours that Grandpa is paying court to the glamorous and wealthy daughter of a local landowner. It is through gentle and self-effacing Grandpa Turvey that the story stretches back in a single generation to a convict ancestor. In fact quiet George Turvey the carpenter seems to have had a motley and amoral selection of relatives, including a brother rumoured to be a horse thief and a sister-in-law who was the unintended victim of a seedy and parochial crime passionel, murdered by her fifteen-year-old brother with a bottle of poisoned whisky. Some Turveys were also apparently no respecters of the barrier of race, for there is evidence of Chinese and Aboriginal liaisons, of which my mother was entirely ignorant until she was an adult. It delighted her that Grandma, that paragon of moral self-righteousness, should have inadvertently attached herself to such a collection of villains and social pariahs.

Connie's boarding house provided a living, and was responsible for my mother's lifelong dislike of housework. It also revealed glimpses of the strange and dangerous adventures of other people's lives. One morning two young men came to the door in great distress, one of them carrying a rifle. They were brothers, and their seventeen-year-old sister had suicided during the night by drinking sulphuric acid. She had been seeing one of the boarders and was pregnant. Grandpa talked quietly to them at the front door while several of the other boarders hustled the offending young man out the back door and away down the railway track.

My mother used to quote a little refrain she had from her mother, who had it from her mother.

Girls keep away from the boys
Give them lots of room
For you ll find when you wed

*They'll hit you on the head
With the bald-headed end of the broom.*

A lively and restless girl in her youth, Connie was still young and attractive when she ran the boarding house. She was determined that her daughters should be educated so they could be independent and would not need to marry. But she did not follow her own advice, and the little rhyme became a self-fulfilling prophecy. She remarried when my mother was in her teens, to one of the boarders who was handsome and charming and spoiled and who believed the only suitable professions for women were nursing and secretarial work. Both girls ran away as soon as they could, my mother to university on a bursary, her younger sister to teachers' college. Their mother eventually escaped from her marriage by going mad in a restrained sort of way and being institutionalised until her death.

The Depression of my mother's childhood is not a place of deprivation and hardship. It is a place in which a young girl with a robust sense of her own potential reluctantly submits to the domestic chores of the boarding house and escapes whenever she can, to the pleasures of playing Tarzan in a tree by the creek and rabbiting among the paddocks. Her other escape is in reading, and she revels in her grandmother's dire predictions that she is just like her feckless father and will come to no good.

The story which she doesn't make much of, but which underpins the other, is of the entrenched narrow-mindedness of a small town in which people are still newcomers after a generation, and a Scotsman like her father is disposed of as a convenient myth once he disappears from the scene. Faint inferences are made about whether he has actually married her mother, and the delicate taint of illegitimacy spices the local gossip. My mother is admonished about some of her friends, whom Connie refers to as 'common'. But her friendship with an itinerant Aboriginal family is not challenged.

My mother's war seems mainly to have consisted of the great lark of air-raids. By this time she was attending boarding school in Perth, and air-raids provided an opportunity to spend hours sauntering about the countryside, pretending not to hear the all-clear when it sounded. A non-Catholic at a Catholic school, she decided early that religion was mostly cant and hypocrisy. She nevertheless attended confirmation classes taught by Canon Bell, having heard a service in which he offered up prayers for the Japanese as well as the Allied dead and grieving, after which most of the congregation walked out. The Canon did not convert my mother, but he provided her with a model of courage and compassion.

The counterpoint to this story is her father's disappearance in Singapore, where he was interned in a POW camp. He subsequently reappeared on an Armistice newsreel, which my mother happened to see as the prelude to a film. He had been largely absent since her early childhood, and his protracted absence during the war did not seem much different. He continued to be an idealised and romantic figure to her, an adventurer who had slipped through the net of ordinariness, and who appeared from time to time on the periphery of her life, illuminated by the glamour of his escape.

In her early twenties my mother's ambition was to travel overseas and to live the exotic and dangerous life of an international spy. To this end she studied Russian and Arabic as extracurricular subjects at university and earned herself an ASIO file, a measure of the government paranoia of the time. Postwar overseas travel was extremely difficult. As a journalist my mother was witness to shiploads of war-shocked refugees, who brought with them stories of places and events that did not mesh with her visions of the exotic and magical. She turned her attention to the exotic that was closer to home, and went north, to the Outback.

It is through my mother's childhood stories that the Australia of the thirties comes alive, the texture and light of the Depression years, the attitudes of small-town rural Australia. My mother's stories are different from my father's. Her presence is often as the protagonist, but she is having an adventure. It is only between the lines that one sometimes glimpses a moment of confusion or fear or loss. She belongs to a generation that does not indulge much in either self-examination or self-pity. The same could be said of my father, but his stories are narrower, deeper, more sensitive and introverted. They are about feelings, perceptions, understandings and aspirations. This boy is familiar to me. I could be this boy.

Between the child my mother and the child me there is a standoff. She is too thick-skinned, too lacking in caution, too embarrassingly herself. She confronts the world with cheerful bravado and regards me, if she regards me at all, with a certain scorn.

AROUND THE FAMILY MEAL TABLE and the station campfires of my childhood I learned the value and the purpose of talk. There was no television. Radio reception was poor and subject to interference. Talk was a major source of entertainment. People told stories in which they won out over villains and fools and circumstance. They told wry and humorous stories in which they lost face, or fights, or money. They told stories of the perfidy, panache and courage of others. They told stories in order to transform the intractable matter of fear and loneliness and failure into something lighter and more flexible. They told themselves into the country.

Often the stories had been told many times, had their own sequence and momentum. The retelling gave things their proper shape and integrity. Within this familiar web new stories found their place. When I left home I took the stories with me. They protected and identified me. They gave me a conviction, which amounted to arrogance, that I came from a world whose values were superior to any I might encounter elsewhere, and concealed, from me at least, the fact that I was afraid of a world in which I might turn out to be no-one at all.

Ironically enough, it was the legacy I inherited from my parents that set me on a track which would inevitably lead me away from their world. They had both left the places they grew up in, had followed the nerve thread which felt like destiny, whatever its risks and unforeseen troubles. In the ethos of my family it was a given that life was a precious adventure, that risks must be taken in the pursuit of dreams. There was no question of settling for conventional choices, an ordinary life. It seems inevitable now that I chose art, which had the stamp of my father's aspirations on it, but which also promised the possibility of finding my private unknown territory. And it did not seem an unreasonably dangerous or threatening place when I first set out to explore it.

But making art involves messing about in dangerous places. It requires you to make yourself open and vulnerable, to listen to the secret anarchic voices which challenge all that is superficial and secondhand. I was locked into the language of my past, a barricade of words which gave my idea of the world its shape. It was a painful process to have it breached. It happened incrementally, at first through the struggle to make work which, if not especially good, at least tried to be honest. I began to glimpse the possibility that the identity I clung to would not serve me. My first response was to pull that identity tightly around me and retreat to the safer ground of developing my skills. But the rift was there, like a road suddenly ripped open by an earthquake. I didn't climb into it willingly. I stayed on the edge until I was flung into it by the most conventional of events, a disastrous love affair.

When I finally crawled out the landscape had changed in all sorts of subtle ways, or the way I saw it had changed, which amounts to the same thing. I had encountered someone in the fault-line whom I didn't know, and whom my own particular set of myths could not accommodate. She crawled out with me, inarticulate and storyless, and although she looked at the world through my eyes, when I tried to speak for her the language was crippled and absurd, full of psychological cliché. Over the years I learned, and am still learning, to listen to her silences. If my own busy voice goes on for too long she begins to howl, a primitive psychic noise which cannot be ignored.

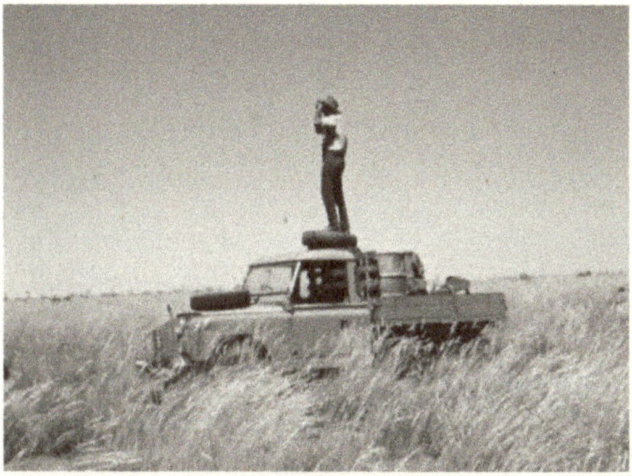

4

I fall from a horse, over and over. In the moment of falling my body is charged electrifyingly with the surge and sweat of the horse, to which I am still linked in a flying arc. For this moment I am raw energy, foam, and sweat, volitionless, a momentum at the extremities of horsepower.

THIS IS LESS A MEMORY THAN an experience I have again and again. When the link breaks and my body flies away from the horse, hits the ground, hurts, collects itself, it turns into memory. But the moment before the link breaks, the sensation of being there, is different in kind from ordinary memory. The story to which I need to give a form is punctuated with charged moments of this nature, which do not lose their intensity with the passage of time.

There is another kind of experience which has also located itself within the unfinished story. At some point in my adult life I became aware of travelling companions. Sometimes I glimpse them in the distance, travelling across my line of vision on some trajectory of their own. At other times I am aware of them as shadows falling just beyond the edge of my conscious mind. Sometimes I encounter them in other people's stories. And sometimes I am travelling with them, their presences as distinct and individual as my own. It is a kind of dreaming, though it does not take place when I am sleeping.

WHEN MY BROTHER BOB RANG me to tell me our father had been killed, I felt as if I had done it. I was working on a series of sculptures and drawings in which I finally felt I had pulled free of my father's influence. The exhibition of the work was to be a declaration to myself of the legitimacy of my own vision. Although I did not expect my father to come to the exhibition, I felt as if I was betraying some old and precious agreement. I did not fully understand the nature of that agreement, I only knew that if my father should see this work he would finally know I was not the daughter he adored, but a stranger whom he neither knew nor understood. It seemed that the curious intensity I had experienced for weeks was the tension of our life threads at cross-purposes, abrading each other, until mine had proved the stronger and cut his through. Although I felt a terrible grief at his death, I felt no guilt. I felt he had given me time, by dying early, to find my own life.

I have two memories of my father's death. There is my own memory, of my brother's voice breaking in the silent grey space of the studio, his words like a physical impact dropping me to my knees.

—Dad's been killed. Helicopter mustering. It crashed. Come as soon as you can.

The seven-hour drive towards a future utterly changed. My mother, so small and terribly crushed.

And there is my brother's memory. He told it to me, and it is as if I am there, running from the gate towards the smashed bubble of the helicopter, hearing the pilot moan, insisting the moan has come from my father even though I know he is dead. I run as one runs in a dream, slower and more slowly, calling my father's name, and the small broken machine recedes and everything is very clear and still. I run and run, and do not get any closer.

Trying to write about him feels the same. Forcing my way through oxygen-deprived air, pushing through the pain barrier with every excrutiatingly slow step. And never getting any closer. But if I was to get close, feel the impact of his personality as I felt it when he was alive, then I could not write at all. The nature of what I am doing is the greatest transgression I can make. I dream often that his death has been temporary, that it was all a mistake. I wake from these dreams in a cold sweat that I have been caught out in my betrayal.

AFTER MY FATHER'S DEATH I began to make maps. To begin with they were dredged up from imagination and a visceral curiosity. Fragments of an imaginary journey, they charted the passage of a mysterious band of travellers, whose existence had first registered as a series of cryptic entries in my artist's journal. The voice which inserted itself into the journal between the rough notations of ideas was the strongest I had yet encountered. Its tone was oddly authoritative, yet full of doubt. The journey it described traversed a landscape which was perfectly familiar to me, but when this strange, faintly prophetic voice took me there, it was as if I had entered a hallucination.

> *The children are beginning to leave. The townspeople have begun to congregate in the square to watch their departure.*

Each morning the crowd is a little larger. Sometimes the horsemen ride out behind the bands of children, and the mud men follow, uttering sad, wild cries like the calling of birds. The horsemen and the mud men return, but the children do not.

The old songs haunt me. I know every track and landmark of the routes which I have never travelled. The green places which the children seek are not a solution. This desert is our place. Our answers are here.

My maps gradually accumulated the evidence of real places and real journeys. I went like a fugitive among my father's papers, finding the maps and journals which were used on that first trip he made through the Tanami. Among them I found a scrap of paper on which he had drawn an early map of the station. Silverfish had nibbled the edges, but the details were intact within the boundaries he had drawn. The neat slanting print transfixed me with the names I remembered so clearly. Madame Pele's Hills, Wild Potato, Lake Ruth, Pedestal Hills, Lucky Bore, the Graveyards, Bullock's Head Lake. And of course the station itself, Mongrel Downs. An ironic joke of a name. Holding the fragment of paper in my hand, I could feel myself disappear into a wilderness of spinifex and claypans and mulga. My father's voice reached out and took hold of me as it had always done. The place and its story seemed to blot out my life, as if nothing had happened to me before or since. And the irony of it was that so little of it was my story.

For a while the map-making concealed the imperative which was slowly building, the need to return to this place whose ambiguous geography haunted me. I did not want to go back. The idea of it filled me with panic. I pretended I did not really have to do it, and began to make left-handed preparations.

5

My first day on the road. Swag, supplies and artist materials are packed on the back of my little yellow Suzuki ute. Sam the dog has made a nest in the spare tyre and has already managed to broach the large bag of dog food that is to last him for the duration of the trip. I am filled with trepidation. It is not the travelling which daunts me, or the being alone. I am afraid of what I will find at the end of the journey.

But it feels good to be heading west, into the heart of the country. My friends who are coastal dwellers feel this when they return to the sea. For me it is the going in that feels right, the further in the better. As the country becomes sparser and redder and drier and stranger, I know that I am getting close to home.

This northern road takes me through remembered country, the windy grasslands, dried out to a palette of umbers and ochres, with the dark blue slash of the bitumen, arrow straight, dividing the horizon at its vanishing point. Trucks float towards me, monstrously tall, reflected in their own mirage. I pass a utility pulled over on the side of the road; a woman is standing some distance away from it, arms folded. A man waits by the open passenger door, his face shadowed under his hat brim. Wedge-tailed eagles rip and nuzzle the swollen corpse of a road kill. The space renders the moment both meaningless and iconic. Cattle graze in pools of light above the horizon. My father, travelling with cattle mobs as a young man, saw windmills suspended upside down over the plains. As I take a bend a line of steel fence-pickets flexes and whips like the tail of a reptile. Along the skyline the grass appears to be running like a herd of small blond animals. It is all illusion and mirage, a place where the imagination cannot outstrip the strange chimerical creations of wind and light and space. It is the kind of country which would take hold of you if you stayed in it for long. In the winter it is riven by bitter winds, and in summer can become a monochrome wasteland. Unrelenting places seem to brand the psyche as gentle green places never can.

The car is hiccupping. It feels like fuel or the electrical system. Problems like this unnerve me. I always feel somehow implicated, as though it is something I've done that has caused the problem. It is bitterly cold, and I can tell already that my cold weather gear won't be sufficient.

I AM BROKEN DOWN BY THE edge of the road among the stony spinifex-covered Mt Isa hills. This is hard, wild country, but its colouring is delicate and full of subtlety. The gums are sharp white, the spinifex blue-green and pale yellow, the stones apricot and pink and terracotta and blood-coloured. The road has been built up here, giving the illusion that the country has been civilised. You have only to step out of sight of the road to know this is not the case.

A big yellow truck comes along and picks up my small

yellow truck. Sam looks alarmed at finding himself suddenly so far off the ground. Ignominiously we return to Mt Isa, where a mechanic replaces the points. Somehow I think the problem is larger than that. I suppose it is an act of folly to set out for the Tanami Desert in a second-hand Suzuki ute which has seen much better days, with a toothless, deaf blue heeler for a companion. But there is no turning back now.

The road between Mt Isa and Camooweal is rough. The new points have not solved the problem, which seems to get worse on rough roads. I stop several times to check the petrol filter and clean the fuel line, and on each occasion a Japanese cyclist I have overtaken catches up and cycles past. On the third occasion he nods and smiles. When I finally reach Camooweal I drain the fuel tank and strain the fuel. I also ask advice from the local mechanic. He is a peeling, ferrety little man who looks as though he has inhaled too many fuel additives. He is supervised by a doting and jealous wife, whom he ignores. If he has any ideas about what is causing the problem, he is keeping them to himself. I decide to keep going, and put my trust in the fact that the Suzuki has never let me down in bad places. It always chooses convenient locations to break down. I have a friend in Alice who will look at it for me, a kind of mechanical magician who will really care about solving the problem.

As I leave Camooweal I see an Aboriginal transvestite standing by the side of the road, apparently waiting for a bus. He is glamorous and unmistakable, with a sinewy brown body and long tawny hair, and is wearing a yellow skirt which reaches his ankles. He is an apparition materialised out of nowhere. The sight of him feels like a good omen. I can't believe that Camooweal could sustain such a life, although the inland is full of surprises, and I am in the border country now. In the past when I have approached Camooweal from the east or west it has been a hallucination of corrugated iron shimmering in and out of focus among dusty earth and white rocks. The Japanese cyclist who kept passing me on the road yesterday is preparing to leave the camp ground and gives me an ironic wave.

Crossing the border back into the Territory, my childhood rushes to meet me. The colours begin to intensify, the light sharpens. I begin to feel something in my bones and nerves and viscera. I would not describe it as an emotion. It is more like a chemical reaction, as if a certain light and temperature and dryness triggers a series of physical and nervous realignments. I stop the car, get out and walk a little distance away from the road. My pulse rate is up, everything takes on a hallucinatory clarity. I sit first, breathing deeply, then stretch full length, inhaling the smell of dry grass and earth, feeling the texture of grains of dirt along my bare arms. It is almost too much, this sense of belonging, of coming home. I roll onto my back and lie staring at the sky, which is punctuated with a few strands of high winter cloud. Sam jumps off the back of the ute, digs himself a hole near the back wheel and settles down to wait.

The great Australian myth of the Outback takes on another dimension here. It is impossible to live in the Territory without being in some way touched by its mythology. It seduces with its hints of the unattainable, the dark heart of the continent, frontier country. Its glamour has been marketed, packaged and sold, and pilgrims come from everywhere to pay homage. But beneath the superficiality of tourist gloss is an older, harder reality. The land here is stronger than the people. Once it has staked its claim, it does not relinquish it.

I lie on the earth and look into the blue immensity of the sky, and the questions ask themselves.

Why can t you live here?
Why did you leave?

When I was a child at boarding school I became aware of the gulf between the city and the bush. Each side held all sorts of derogatory assumptions about the other. The city was a stinking, crowded, polluted hotbed of ill-informed left-wing intellectuals, politicians and conservationists. It was a place of crime, corruption and distrust, where neighbours didn't speak to one another and you couldn't let your kids play in the streets. City people were swayed by the fickle winds of media opinion, out of touch with practical realities and addicted to material excess and soft living.

The country, on the other hand, was an intellectual desert full of bigots, racists and rednecks who bulldozed the last existing stands of ancient forest through pure bloody-mindedness. If they no longer organised hunting parties to shoot down Aborigines, they still thought it was a good idea. The macho ideals of manhood ruled supreme, shored up by alcohol and violence. Country people were ill-informed, unsophisticated, attached to a romanticised notion of rugged individualism and resistant to change and new ideas.

There was an additional element in the urban view of the country. At a certain point it ceased to be the country and became the Outback, a mythical zone of spiritual possibilities and marvellous landscape. It harboured primordial secrets, and it cast a curious grace on all those who lived in it or passed through it.

It took me a long time to shed the attitudes of my own childhood. I discovered that I loved cities, the bigger the better. I even enjoyed the company of left-wing intellectuals. My own attitudes and values were challenged continually, and while I did not abandon them I modified them radically.

And yet there was something missing in the assessment my city friends made of the country. There was little understanding of a dignity, an integrity, a stoic perseverance that seemed to me admirable even when it was attached to opinions I no longer shared. And there was a romanticism, a sentimentality in relation to the landscape and the Aborigines, which also sat uncomfortably, and which had nothing to do with the reality of what I remembered.

As long as I stay away from the country I grew up in, I can manage these contradictions. When I come back to it I feel like an imposter. The people of the world to which I once belonged treat me as if I am one of them, assume that I understand the intricacies and difficulties of their lives as no outsider can. And of course I do. I am sucked back into the world which shaped me, with its harsh imperatives, its black humour and subtle understandings. It reclaims me, and the divisions no longer exist outside me but are inside, laying equal claim on my allegiances.

It is simply too uncomfortable. I cannot resolve the contradictions. In fact I don't believe they should be resolved. This is an age when such contradictions are the reality of the time. I have neither the physical stamina nor the moral fibre to live all the time with them actively confronting each other. I can manage it for short bursts, and then I must retreat to where the turmoil can settle and the ambiguities transform themselves into a creative tension with which I can engage.

There is no middle ground. In the softer coastal fringes I found something flexible and cosmopolitan which felt like another sort of homecoming. But there is no substitute for the true inland, the edge of the desert.

THE OLD ROADHOUSES OF Barry Caves and Frewena are gone, replaced by a great green glossy BP service station with a shop full of tourist bric-a-brac. I refuel and drive on a few kilometres before pulling off the road to brew coffee. Intellectually I appreciate the surrealism of these space stations in the landscape, and no doubt they are more efficient than their predecessors; but their ugliness, inside and out, has a stridency which distresses me.

Across the Barkly Tablelands the dark blue bitumen road goes on forever, until it hits the T-junction of the Three Ways. Somebody once told me of directions given to a family who had arrived by ship in Perth and whose final destination was Townsville. Go straight ahead until you get to Port Augusta. Turn left and keep going until you reach Three Ways. Then turn right and keep going until you hit the coast.

The car seems to be okay as long as I don't go over ninety kilometres per hour. All afternoon the sky around the sun has been a curious pinkish colour, striped with indigo clouds. As I turn left at Three Ways, perpendicular ranks of cloud begin to march at great speed. The sky blazes into a sunset so spectacular it is absurd, and I drive laughing into a flamboyance of gold and bronze and pink and silver and fathomless blue.

I camp at the Devil's Marbles, which have been fenced in. There is a designated camp ground and I follow the signs obediently. The old anarchic days when we pulled off the side of the road, threw down our swags and camped where we liked are over. The camp ground is neatly demarcated with a low timber railing, and for a moment I think I have arrived on another planet. I am in a village of white four-wheel drives and white caravans, and no people. The sun has gone, and the great piles of granite stones hold the light, releasing it slowly. There is a hum of generators. Inside the caravans I can see the flicker of television screens. Here in the sublime dusk a mobile suburbia has come to a halt.

Sam goes off to pee on the wondrous array of car and caravan wheels while I light a fire and drop the side of the utility tray out into a ready-made kitchen bench. Here and there a face moves across the yellow light of a window, watching, as I prepare my meal by the light of the slowly dimming stones. Later a battered and overloaded station wagon pulls in, carrying three raffish-looking kids. They drag blankets and bundles out of the vehicle and crawl off among the rocks to sleep. I am glad of them and their disregard of fences and prohibitions.

6

IT IS A BRIGHT WINTER DAY when I arrive in Alice. The air is sharp and luminous. If I have a home town, it is Alice Springs. It contains for me the childhood memories I recognise in Australian writers, the petty classroom cruelties, the sound of crows, the smell of asphalt and dust, the notion that some sinister grace separates Catholics from non-Catholics.

I came here as a seven year old, when the population was about three thousand. Today there are traffic lights at the causeway crossing of the Todd River, but the air has the same crisp eucalypt smell I remember. We used to stand on the footbridge when the Todd came down, egging on adventurous and foolhardy drivers to make a dash before the river got too high. Someone always took up the challenge and more often than not was washed off the causeway, becoming the centre of a major rescue operation. We took this as a personal achievement. The river used to come down in a tumbling creamy flood, with a head of foam on it like a schooner of freshly pulled beer. For a few days the town side and the East side would be divided. School would be disrupted as the Aboriginal students from St Mary's hostel and kids from the

Gap and the industrial area couldn't make it across the river to the East side school.

But it happened all too rarely in those years of entrenched, continual drought. Mostly we rode our bicycles across the dusty flat to the school, barefoot and scabby-kneed, attuned as lizards to our arid world. All the years of my childhood were dry years. Old people talked of a green time when the rainfall in a year was twenty-five inches and more. We drought children did not believe them. Our reality was of dust storms turning the sky into a red dome, and of scalded-looking yards of yellow grass and the wide dry sandy bed of the Todd River. The green years came back in the seventies, but it is impossible to put aside the sense that drought is the true condition of this country, that the sudden bursts of rainfall and growth are cosmetic and transient.

I take a turn after the causeway crossing and drive along the street we lived in. It is much shorter than I remembered, the encircling ranges closer, pinker and higher. The river red gum seedlings my father planted thirty years ago dominate the street. I look at the house as it stands now, ramshackle and overshadowed by the big red gums, the oleander hedge luxuriant and poisonous. In the back yard, which I can't see, lurks the furred, malevolent presence of my first horse, an evil Shetland named Happy. Even now the word carries overtones for me of the rolled-back white of an eye and something subversive and unpredictable.

I can see my mother crouching with a broomstick, trying to prize my brother out from the brick chimney foundation under the house. She is howling threats as to what she will do to him when she gets hold of him. He scuttles out of the alcove and deep into the spider-infested darkness under the house. At this point my mother abandons the broom and begins shying rocks in an attempt to flush him out. It is quite probable that I am standing by handing the rocks to her. He makes a sudden dash and escapes over the back fence, my mother close behind, yelling—Wait till I catch you, you bloody little swine!

These are the days when my brother Bob and I are arch enemies. He can reduce me to a blind, murderous rage simply by pulling faces, and because he is small and very fast I rarely catch him. I revenge myself after nightfall, when he is in the outdoor lavatory with the car lights switched on to illuminate the dark stretch of the back yard. He has invented a kind of monster called a gark, and these cluster in the smelly darkness of the lavatory. I dash out and flick off the lights and scream—Garks! at the top of my voice, and my brother howls with terror and bolts for the safety of the house.

THE RANGE TO THE SOUTH of the town has subtleties of texture and colour that seduce and excite my painter's eye. This aesthetic response drives home to me the fact that I have been away too long. There was a time when the notion of beauty would not have entered my head, when it was simply my place. I did not know it was beautiful, but I knew the bends in the riverbed and the stony tracks and gorges through the hills. Even now my memories are of the way the shadows fell on rock, and the way the dust came up over the ranges like red smoke.

Now I pay homage like any other stranger.

MY FRIEND PAM LIVES ON THE East side, in a part of Alice Springs which has not changed much, although the saltbush and claypan area we called the Swamp has been built on, and the dusty flat near the school is a grassy playing field.

In Pam's yard the citrus trees are laden with fruit, thin-skinned mandarins and the addictively sweet oranges which grow here. The scent of oranges assails me with nostalgia. In the morning the sun filters through slatted blinds and strikes bands of light on the yellow wall. This is the light I remember from childhood. I took it for granted, that such light was a part of life, that light and space were a given.

A small green and grey bird is bouncing in the terracotta birdbath. His voice is very big and resonant for such a small bird, a three-syllable statement made with great emphasis. He falls backwards into the birdbath, and flies away in a flurry at my burst of laughter. Today for the first time in months I feel no anxiety. Something has lifted, this light has got through. In between the hard new shapes the old town survives. It is the light which draws it all together and makes it a town I can remember.

Pam is an artist whose personal philosophy places her very much on the side of the Aboriginal community and against the pastoral industry and what it stands for. To her I can speak about the contradictions and difficulties which confront me, but nevertheless they remain as acknowledged differences between us that push me sometimes into defensiveness and irritation. Last night we talked about the culture of the town. Of course we talked about Aborigines, and of course I sounded off with all sorts of opinions. I woke up this morning thinking—*Shut up, Kim.*

I get in touch with my friend the mechanic, who identifies the problem with the car as a worn distributor spline. The morning is spent tracking down a second-hand distributor, which he installs for me.

Tomorrow I go north-west.

MOST OF MY VERY EARLY memories are of travelling through an essentially flat landscape, studded with patches of low scrub, sometimes with grass, sometimes without, and always somewhere on the horizon a blue range or escarpment or series of hills. The colour would deepen to purple as we got closer and then turn into flat-topped red sandstone or green and yellow spinifex cover or something equally unpredictable. Slowly the mysterious, uniform, transparent blue that was only slightly deeper in intensity than the sky would solidify, become opaque and textured. Details would emerge, a watercourse or track, vegetation, rocks, colours, an accumulation and refinement of texture which obliterated the dreamlike distance. When I remembered to do it, I would turn and watch as we travelled past and away, until the range or hill was reclaimed by distance and retreated again into the transparent realms of possibility and imagination.

The range which today cuts its blue template along the western horizon is the Stuart Bluff Range. It lies like a series of wedges, end to end, making a tidy saw-toothed edge of the horizon. Mt Wedge Station is named for the highest of the hills, Central Mt Wedge. It was owned by one of the original members of the stock route land party, Bill Waudby, and is run now by his son. I make camp along the turnoff track and puncture a tyre when I pull off the road into the mulga scrub. There is still plenty of light, so I unload some gear and change the tyre, to save doing it in the morning. I could call in and see Bob Waudby, whom I knew when we were children, and who I know would make me feel welcome. But I feel introspective, unable to make the effort required for social interaction. It is as if I must hoard my emotional energy for whatever it is that I am going to encounter. There was never any doubt in my mind that this journey must be made alone, but it leaves Sam as my only outlet for light relief, and tonight he is not providing it. We sit in silence by the campfire, and the night is very cold and big around us.

7

THIS MORNING, BETWEEN THE Mt Wedge turnoff and Yuendumu, I am hailed by two Aboriginal men with a battered white car. They are pulled over on the side of the road with the bonnet up. On this track we never ignored someone in trouble, and old habits die hard. Of course I have been told all the horror stories of white women being raped by black men, but I pull over anyway. This morning I don't feel like a potential rape victim. There are no pleasantries exchanged. They simply ask me for some motor oil. I give them enough to get to Yuendumu, as I am only carrying enough for my own trip. The taller of the two is the spokesman. He doesn't look at me when he speaks. The next demand is for a 'tin o' meat', so I give him a packet of corned beef from the esky. When he produces an empty water container from the car I start to grin. It is just as well this is not a first, romanticised encounter with the desert Aborigine. I fill the water container and leave them to get themselves going. There are lots of vehicles along this road these days, so I am not concerned about them breaking down again.

Driving away, I am curious about the dynamics of the

encounter. I was not at all afraid, partly because I have known and worked with many Aboriginal men. But I think too there is an element of 'white missus' in my thinking, an assumption that we inhabit mutually exclusive worlds, which is a hangover from my past. I wonder if I would have stopped for two white men looking as disreputable. Probably not.

I go in to Yuendumu to get the spare mended. At the garage the mechanic who mends the tyre is curious about my destination. When I tell him Mongrel Downs he says— I did some work out there a few years ago. It was a hundred and twenty in the shade. Hellhole of a place. I could see why they called it Mongrel Downs.

When Mongrel Downs was first named, the administrator of the Northern Territory, who had been obstructive in the granting of the lease, thought it had been named after him. More recently an Aboriginal friend sent me a newspaper cutting describing the transfer of the station into Aboriginal hands and its subsequent renaming as Tanami Downs. The article suggested that the old name was an example of the attitude previous white owners had had towards the country, and the renaming was a mark of respect. An artist friend in Alice who works for the sacred sites department tells me that the local Aborigines believe Mongrel is a distortion of Monkarrurpa, which is the traditional name for Lake Ruth. In a Brisbane gallery I picked up a catalogue of work by Balgo and Tanami artists, and featured in it was a work by a woman artist from 'Mongrelupa'.

In fact the naming was an ironic response to local scepticism. The popular perception of the Tanami was that it was an uninhabitable desert region, and the general consensus was that Joe Mahood and Bill Wilson must be mad to try to create a cattle station on 'that mongrel bit of country out there'. So Bill and my father called it Mongrel Downs as a kind of up-yours gesture.

The first white man to have traversed and mapped the country was Allan Arthur Davidson, surveyor and geologist, aged twenty-two or thirty-one. He notes in his report on the expedition he led into the region he called the Tanami, after the Aboriginal name for a site of permanent rockholes:

> Between latitude 20 and 21 degrees, and longitude 129 degrees, we struck a splendid belt of pastoral country, the only good country of its sort we sighted on the whole trip.

The Davidson report was filed and forgotten in the archives of the South Australian Lands Department, his 'splendid belt of pastoral country' existing briefly as a rumour and then disappearing from memory.

It is strange to be on this road again. I remember each landmark as it comes up, though they seem to have become slightly rearranged. The road has been well maintained since the reopening of the Tanami and Granites goldfields, so it is in much better shape than the track we used to travel in the sixties. At Chilla Well a loop of the old track has been cut off, and I follow it. This is the road I remember, red wheel-tracks up a limestone rise and the bloodwood tree with the carved trunk overlooking the bore. The tanks are rusting now, the windmill creaks occasionally into the wind but pumps no water. The stock-route bores have all fallen into disuse.

The old Mongrel Downs turnoff is marked by two steel signposts without signs. Of the track itself there is no trace, although I walk in a hundred yards or more searching for it. These days the access road cuts back south-west from Rabbit Flat. I plan to call in to Rabbit Flat, but the roadhouse is closed for three days a week and doesn't reopen until tomorrow, so tonight I will camp along the track.

THIS FIRST NIGHT IN THE Tanami feels very benign and familiar. My campsite is of red earth and soft wheat-coloured grasses, spinifex and the elegant small desert gums with their white trunks and deep green furry leaves. The giant anthills are the most striking feature of this part of the country. They hulk across the landscape, almost animate, each with an individual weirdness of shape that hints at sentience, at some kind of purposefulness in their design. There is a steady light wind blowing, which is causing the fire to flame up. I was lucky to find enough wood for a fire, the remains of a solid, partly burned log, as the white ants consume every bit of dead wood almost instantly. The sun went down quickly, and the kerosene lantern is hissing softly, the only sound apart from the movement of grass in the wind.

I have never been alone out here in quite this way. When I lived here there was always the family, the people who worked for us, the central focus of the homestead. All my solitary wandering moved out from a fixed, inhabited point. Now I am moving through it like a stranger, unsure of why I am really here, driven by some imperative I don't fully understand.

My father loved to be alone in this country. I think he felt safe in it, away from other people. This is a legacy I have inherited from him. I think one of the reasons I have come back here is to try to discover what is me and what is him, and to separate them as best I can. What I do know is that this place is an integral part of the equation.

The country exists apart from all this stuff I am investing in it. It is separate from the memories, the attachments, the mythology. Coming back to it makes me remember this. The place in my head is not and never was this place. For moments at a time I am simply here. The wind which moves quietly in the grass is the same wind which moves across time and through my mind, leaving a clear emptiness behind it.

I wake before daylight and watch the eastern horizon brighten slowly. It is suddenly colder, with the dawn chill that marks the last ditch of the night. Sam has complained so bitterly of the cold that I have made him a nest in the cabin of the Suzuki, warning him that this is not to become a habit. The sun comes up like the top of a forty-four gallon drum and rolls on the flat edge of the desert. A few scattered bird calls acknowledge it, but for the most part the bush is perfectly still.

I am on the road early and pass the signs for the Granites goldmine. They warn of danger and no public access. This was the point where my father's party left the beaten track and went west.

The stock-route party carried with them the maps and a segment of the journal kept by Allan Davidson, the only official documentation of a previous traverse of the Tanami region. The diary segment is a yellowing photocopy of a typed copy of the original. It begins at Camp 53, Monday, July 23rd, 1900, at which point Allan Davidson has crossed into Western Australia, and ends at Camp 78, Friday, August 31st, 1900, somewhere in the region of the Smoke Hills south of the Tanami rockholes. It has been among my father's papers for years. I have glanced at it from time to time, unable to muster the incentive to penetrate the blurred print and technical terminology. But now, persevering, I find myself slowly drawn in, because I can imagine how it was for him to see the country for the first time, this country that I am travelling through, remembering my own experience of seeing it for the first time, remembering my father's description of seeing it for the first time. Davidson came upon the

Granites from the west, having travelled to the Western Australian border along a route much further to the north. The Granite Hill, as he named it, was one of the last points he discovered before heading homewards.

> Camp No 71. Sunday, August 19th, 1900.
> From this ridge the blackish hill for which we had taken our bearing loomed up prominently to the eastward ... Byrne had preceded us to this hill, and was to send up a smoke if he sighted water. A smoke went up shortly afterwards, so we continued our course to the hill ... On his arrival Byrne saw a native, but he disappeared shortly afterwards, and did not again honour us ...
>
> Good camel feed is abundant, consisting of munyaroo, bluebush, and various other dainty varieties of herbage ... Jack (the blackboy) discovered a rockhole containing an abundant supply of water ... Byrne managed to shoot a wallaby this evening, so we now live in anticipation of some fresh stew. This appeared to be the last wallaby in the hill, and as he is small, the natives had probably left him to develop.

Among my father's papers is a slide taken at the Granites on the return journey he made with Bill Wilson and Milton Willick. Bill sits in the roofless cabin of a rusting vehicle, his hands on the steering wheel and his hat pulled rakishly over one eye. Behind him is the skeletal silhouette of a windmill, and scattered about on the stony ground are the remnants of abandoned mine workings. Although it is a colour slide it gives the impression of a sepia image, the landscape is so bleached and monochromatic. It strikes me as a quintessentially Australian image in its depiction of the iconography of failed enterprise, its humorous irony and the sheer nondescript desolation of the landscape.

New technology and good roads have made the mine viable again, and as I drive past I can hear the faint grind of heavy equipment burrowing and pulverising and processing. I spare a thought for Byrne's solitary native, disappearing from the granite hill as a man on a camel appears on the skyline.

At Rabbit Flat I renew my acquaintance with Bruce and Jackie Farrands, who met each other on Mongrel Downs in my family's time and established the roadhouse shortly before we left the country. They are a kind of landmark now, having done their time and earned their place in the country.

I ring the manager of Tanami Downs to let him know I will be arriving sometime during the morning. The wide red road which links Rabbit Flat and Tanami Downs surprises me, though of course it should not. It provides access to Dead Bullock gold mine, which is on the ancestral route between Tanami and Inningarra. The traditional owners of the country receive royalties from the mine.

Between Rabbit Flat and Mongrel (I must remember to think of it as Tanami) Downs, runs a string of fresh and saltwater claypans. Davidson notes the nature of the country as he passes this way, describing claypans crusted with a fine salt, and dried-up marshland scattered with the small tough vegetation known as samphire. There is a glimpse of the old story in his language, the dream of an inland sea which tormented a generation of explorers.

> ... and so where sheets of water had in days gone by brightened the features of a dead country there now exists this peculiar belt of country, which cannot be described as a lake and only barely comes under the heading of a marsh.

In the days before the track existed, we used to follow the edge of the claypans and come out on the Tanami road south of the present location of Rabbit Flat. I remember travelling back just on sundown, picking the track we had made by the different way the light fell on the bent grass, glimpsing the marks of tyre treads here and there on patches of sandy soil.

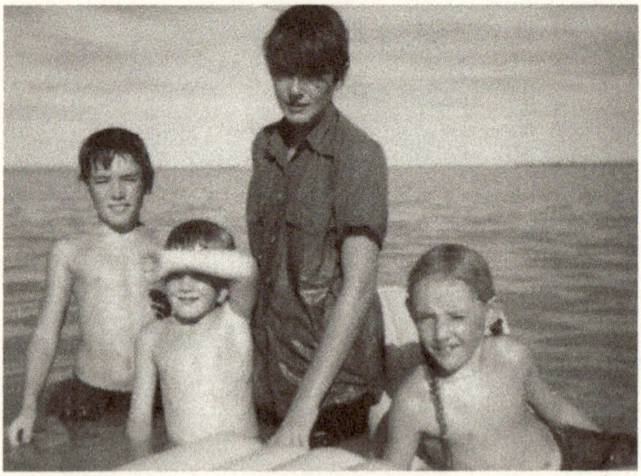

8

I AM SHAKEN BY MY INITIAL encounter with the homestead. Some of it is very changed, some of it disturbingly familiar. It is impossibly strange to be here. I feel as if I have walked into my own past and found myself to be absent from it. I feel like a phantom, an animated absence whose identity is contained in the yellow Suzuki.

I drink tea with the manager, whose wife and children are away at a pony club meeting, and discuss my plans for spending some time driving around the station. Adam is employed by the Aboriginal owners to manage the property and has been here with his family for several years. He gives me a recent map, with new bores and tracks and fence lines. Within the net of new lines I can see the simpler tracery of what I remember.

The homestead has been painted white and is fenced in with a neat yard of lawns, cedar trees and bougainvillea. There is even a swimming pool. It is as if a kind of green band has been established between the bush and the homestead, a narrow zone of emigrant trees and artificial tidiness. When we lived here the building perched like a tent in the mulga, more like a permanent campsite than a serious homestead. The clear images of memory slide in and out of focus. As I walk around I register gaps, intrusions. The windmill has gone, and with it the creak and whirr of the blades that was as familiar a sound as the wind itself. The overhead tank is still here, with the narrow metal ladder I climbed as a child when I needed to test my courage. The big bough shed which was the first campsite and later the five-star chook pen has gone, and so has the orchard of citrus trees so carefully nurtured by my father. I am surprised to discover that I am crying. A chained blue heeler watches me beadily, and Sam grumbles at him from the back of the ute.

The interior of the homestead has been modified so that the basic design of a central rectangle of rooms surrounded by a wide flywired verandah has almost disappeared. It has the feeling of a real house instead of the adapted shearers' quarters of the original design. The place is much changed, but the same single beds occupy the verandah. In the living room there is now a television set. There are also two green vinyl armchairs. The sight of them, more particularly the vinyl smell of them, transfixes me in the centre of the rather nondescript room. Outside, the crisp winter light breaks into patterns among the cedars and bougainvillea.

THE GIRL RETREATS FROM the afternoon heat and persistent flies to the living room of the half-finished house. She has unearthed *Hatter's Castle* from a carton of paperback novels abandoned by some passing traveller. It is the summer before she goes away to boarding school, and she is spending the holidays with her father on the station. Her mother will not move the family out here until the house is finished.

In the uninhabitable hours of the afternoon the girl reads. It is a dark tale, of fathers and daughters and betrayal and tragedy. The green armchair in which she curls gives off the smell of sweaty vinyl, an ochre-coloured smell that sticks in the back of the throat and leaves an aftertaste. Outside the dark cave of the room the afternoon looms like a hallucination. It is that time of day when the light presses everything flat and there are no shadows. The mulga gives off a faint but perceptible acacia stink.

She has set herself the task of climbing the overhead tank later in the day when the light is friendly. The tank is very high, almost as high as the windmill, and she is afraid of it. When she saw it she wished she did not have to climb it, but the harder she wished it the more she knew she would have to do it. Now it is simply a matter of getting it over with.

The old man who is finishing the interior of the house is a compulsive talker and inflicts on anyone who will listen the story of his life, which is a meandering and pointless invention of almost lunatic banality. At first, conscious of the respect due him as an adult, the girl listens, but she soon learns to retreat into her book and shut him out, as everyone shuts him out. Days go by when no-one allows him to speak to them, for fear of triggering the unquenchable flow of words. She would avoid him altogether if she could, but the house is the only place where she can escape from the flies. In the end the flies and the dangers of the overhead tank are preferable to the whining drill of his voice. She can still hear him talking as she scampers across the hot red ground.

From the top of the overhead tank she has a view out across the mulga scrub to the north and west of the homestead. To the east she can see the red spinifex country with the giant anthills, right out to where the country changes colour and begins to drop away towards the shallow basin of Lake Ruth. There is a long blue hill on the eastern horizon, and a line of trees to the south which indicate a watercourse. From her vantage point she can look directly down onto the green circle of the stock tank and the roof of the bough shed. The smoke from the campfire winds a blue ribbon above the mulga. The camp cook potters about, stoking the fire under the beef bucket, mixing a damper, filling the flat-sided billycans. She wishes she had a shanghai to ping him with. He would never look for her up here. Now she has climbed the tank she is not at all afraid and is reluctant to relinquish this bird's-eye view. She can see the old man sawing wood on the verandah of the house. Malley and the black stockmen are cleaning up around the shed, the small busy figures carrying bits of steel and timber. She sleeps outside, and she imagines floating down slowly and coming to rest in the middle of her bed. Further away the dunny sits in the middle of the flat, with a piece of hessian draped around a few pickets for modesty's sake. It is a forty-four gallon drum sunk in the ground, a hole cut in the top with an oxy torch. For most of the daylight hours it is too hot to sit on, so everyone goes bush.

There is a line of dust coming up along the track from the west, her father and Ferdie coming back from checking a site to drill for water. Ferdie is Austrian, and teases her, calling her the little skinny witch with the long skinny legs.

She is very content in this world. She is no-one's older sister here, there are no domestic chores for which she is responsible, there is no domesticity to speak of. Every few days when she feels grubby she washes herself, her hair and her clothes in the cattle trough. Most days she rides out bareback on the piebald horse she has been given and explores the surrounding mulga scrub and the claypan country.

Sometimes the camp is moved for a few days to one of the bores, and the cattle are mustered and branded. Then life becomes even simpler, though harder.

The girl absorbs this perspective of the world which is her father's world, which is to become her world. The late afternoon light fills it with colour. She can smell the woodsmoke of the campfire. From here she owns it all.

LATER, WHEN I DRIVE TO Lake Ruth, the sense of dislocation is even more intense. A dreamy suntanned teenager dogs my footsteps as I walk to the clump of ti-tree at the edge of the big white claypan. It is dry, as it was when the light plane carrying my father and four others attempted to land on it thirty years ago, crashing instead, with miraculously no serious injuries. The topography is utterly familiar. The boat is still here. My father brought it back from Adelaide and we all learned to sail. It lies like an abandoned folly on the edge of the dry lake. If I am looking for an icon for my trip this has to be it. A craft for a dry lake, a vessel to carry the detritus of memory, marooned in the desert light.

The rusting remains of the raft some visiting friends built is still here too, in scattered fragments across the lake bed. It is all instantly familiar, and yet it resists memory. It will not receive the load of the past I want to dump onto it. I am standing on the rim of a remote, low-lying claypan surrounded by ti-tree scrub and spinifex. Its dry surface is powdered with cattle tracks, a strong wind blowing gusts of white dust. It reduces me to a kind of suffocating anguish, and I crouch for a long time in the sand among the ti-tree. The flies are bad, but not as bad as I remember, probably because of the dry years.

After a time I collect myself and walk across the bed of the lake to the little creek my brother Bob and I named Flint Creek one afternoon many years ago. Sam the dog is a little uneasy and sticks close, a pace or two behind me. The flints are lying about everywhere, as I remembered, and I pocket a couple of reddish golden flakes to take back for my brother.

A DREAM. A MEMORY. AN AFTERNOON.

The water splashes softly around the oars, creamy, pale brown, the colour of milky tea. Nothing but the small boat moves through all this stillness of water and sunlight. The two in the boat are mesmerised by the slow dipping of the oars. The creak of oars, the soft splash of water is the only language of this sun-stunned, emptied afternoon.

Beneath the membrane that divides above from below is an opaque blind turbulent place. They have been there and encountered mud and swimming things and each other's flailing limbs. It is not dark, but pale and luminous, and yet one can see nothing. It is full of eyeless, mud-dwelling, scaly things. They watch themselves and the boat mirrored in the shining opaque surface of the lake. They are castaways ... sharks nudging their makeshift raft ... days since they have had fresh water to drink ... nothing to eat but a raw and stringy seabird, a cormorant, the boy thought, which they managed to trap and strangle. The sun beats down, there is no chance of rescue, they are dying ...

They have not noticed the creek before, meandering its shallow course between spinifex and ti-tree to the lake's edge. This requires a new game, a shift of mood. Intrepid, fearless, they turn their sturdy boat towards the mouth of this great river. Wild savages inhabit the dense jungle along its banks, anacondas and alligators writhe in the shallows. They land the boat with a flurry, dodging reptile coils and fangs. On the white sand lie fragments of worked stone, razor-edged flakes the colour of rust and amber. The boy picks up one of these and makes cutting motions with it, scoring marks in the soft sand. The older child, the girl, sits cross-legged and fits cores and flakes together, then strikes them apart again, searching about in the sand for the stone tools necessary for the task. They gather up these pieces of coloured stone and pile them together. Each stone contains its own mystery, holding in itself the memory of the other hands which have held and crafted and discarded it. The children run fingers and thumb over scooped surfaces and serrations and curves, and measure the weight and shape and warmth of stone in the palms of their hands. They take up their piles of treasure and scatter them again onto the sand.

The light is changing. Beyond the circle of ti-tree the ant-hills cast lengthening shadows. The explorers launch their boat onto the river and paddle out into the great still expanse of the lake. The marauding Tanamites are threatening from the east, looming in the guise of giant anthills, red and lumpish, rank upon rank of them right back to the horizon. The children paddle desperately in the creamy water, trying to reach the safety of their campsite on the western shore. The Tanamites cannot cross water. The lake will hold them back.

The girl is bemused by this boy who is her brother. He has an unself-conscious curiosity which allows him to engage with the world in a way she cannot. He is alive with an extraordinary intelligent energy and goes headlong from moment to moment with a kind of fearless glee. Since she has gone away to school they no longer fight. With her absence he has grown into his own place, and those passionate fierce sibling battles no longer have any point. She has discovered instead that they share a kind of leaping imagination, a delight in this world which is their own place, a language which is largely without words, which is the language of the country.

They make a campfire before the sun goes down and put the billy on to boil. Dingoes come to drink a little distance from the camp, their coats reddish-gold in the late afternoon light. The waterbirds make a great to-do about the day coming to an end. The lake turns deep pink and then dulls to violet, and the evening star makes its appearance in a sky of the same colour. The children are quiet as the daylight fades, busying themselves with preparations for the night, building the fire up against the encroaching darkness. They poke potatoes into the coals to bake and fry chunks of steak on the flat of a shovel. The night is moonless, and as the sky darkens the stars come on as if a million switches have been flicked. The Southern Cross is up there, and the Saucepan, and the soft luminosity of Magellan's Cloud. The Milky Way looks like the shining wake of space dust raised by a racing mob of horses. The children imagine their counterparts, somewhere out there on one of those spinning stars, sitting beside their own lake and looking out across the same universe.

They assure each other that the Tanamites are safely held back by the far shore of the lake, then crawl into their swags, to sleep cradled in the white sand among the protective shrubbery of ti-tree.

I WILL HAVE TO SPEND TIME and camp here. There is something unnerving about finding the lake still here. For a long time it has existed only in my imagination. Now its familiar contours hold the traces of a remembered time far more intensely than I have ever imagined. And yet its realness simultaneously displaces memory, insists on the passage of time which has separated me from place and memory. I sense something of the impulse which drives the Aborigines to revisit sites, to reinvest them with the meanings and memories necessary to make them habitable. It is one thing to keep a place alive in the mind, another to go back to that place and hold both past and present together. I pull my swag off the back of the vehicle and unroll the white groundsheet. Already it is beginning to accumulate the dirt and marks of the journey. It is almost the same colour as the pale sand. I mark a rectangle in its centre, drawing the boundaries of this country to which I have returned, formal, fictional, necessary boundaries which are no more than a convention, a point of departure. Using a wash of dark pigment I fill the rectangle, crawling about on hands and knees, spreading the black stain across the canvas. The thoughtless, repetitious action is a relief, a respite from thinking. My shadow intercedes between me and the work.

A shadow moves too on the lake surface, though when I turn to see what casts it, there is nothing. Only the echo of a presence I have glimpsed before, moving through the pages of my journal.

> *The windy days are the most difficult, the dust gets into eyes and mouth and nostrils, and the wind blows away the drawings on the lake surface before they are even completed. The maps must be redrawn daily. The half-erased maps of the windy days are a measure of the lives we now lead, moving aimlessly about the perimeters of the lake systems, adrift somewhere between the memory of a nomadic past and the dream of a transformative future.*
>
> *Sometimes this temporary nature of the maps suggests the*

fragility and impermanence of our way of life. And sometimes it seems like an act of faith, a folly which celebrates each moment in which the marks are made, exist and fade. There are times when I am alone, far out on the lake surface, when I feel as if the bones in my body are continuous with the stratas of limestone which break through the surface of the country, when my blood is the same as the salty fluid that still runs between veins of rock beneath the surface, when my teeth and hair and nails are the brittle grasses and ti-tree scrub which grow about the rim of the lake. It feels as if the lake dust holds the substance of all the people who have made the journeys I write into its surface, as if every particle of dust is a word from the songs.

The wind has blown lake sand across the wet pigment, blurring the edges of the boundaries I have drawn. The shadows are growing longer. It is time to go.

9

My memory of tracks runs as deep as an instinct. I feel my way towards the sites I remember, and they are still there. I drive back from Lake Ruth along the sandy wheel tracks of the old road, searching for the track to Dakoty Bore, which is on a small watercourse south of the homestead. In good seasons there is a waterhole in the creek bed. This is the next point after Lake Ruth on the track between Tanami and Inningarra. It has another name, an Aboriginal name which I don't know. But I do know how it came to be called Dakoty.

It is Christmas Eve, and the children have rigged makeshift lighting and some props on the back lawn. They have discovered an obscure recording on the flip-side of an EP and are entranced by it. They have been quoting from it for days. A small stretch of the imagination transforms the scene into a Western bar-room, with a small blonde bartender, an androgynous teenage cowboy and a tiny bearded old man. A dog lounges at the foot of the bar. A small dapper figure in a very large hat struts into the bar and announces himself.

—Howdy, barkeep. They call me the Denver Dragon. I'm a-lookin for a feller named Billy the Kid.

The bartender glances at the cowboy, who makes no move, and answers the newcomer.

—I heared he was waay up in Dakoty.

The Dragon struts and preens, orders drinks all round, and proceeds to outline what he will do to Billy the Kid when he finds him. He lets it be known that he is a dangerous customer with a string of dead outlaws to his credit. Tiny Granpaw in his cotton-wool beard downs his whisky and watches the Dragon with bright sceptical eyes. The bartender plays along, bats eyelids and murmurs—You must have a mighty lot of notches on your gun.

—Lady, I got so many notches on my gun I just natcherly whittled the handle plumb away.

The Dragon, gratified with his captive audience, including the group of adults on the perimeter of the lawn, hams outrageously. He sidles up to the silent cowboy at the bar.

—What's your name, small fry?

There are a few snorts from the audience, since he is not much over waist high on the cowboy.

—William Bonney.

—William Bonney! Now ain't that just the sweetest name.

—Some folks call me . . . Billy the Kid.

Granpaw chortles and scampers up onto the bar for a better view, utterly carried away by the drama of it all. The bartender swats at him, angel face bright.

—B . . . B . . . Billy the Kid! But I heered you was waay up in Dakoty!

—I was in Dakoty. I'm here now.

The Kid is relishing the deadpan, laconic role.

—W ... W ... Why Billy, I'm mighty pleased to meet you. I been wantin' to make your aquaintance for a long time.

—That's what I heered you say a while ago.

—Aw Billy, I was just foolin'.

—Well I ain't!

Billy pulls her gun and aims at the Dragon's feet. Granpaw whoops and does a war dance on the bar and the bartender puts the bottles out of harm's way. The Denver Dragon howls and dances across the lawn to the accompaniment of cap-gun reports, and the dog gets into the act by trying to bite Billy. The audience roars and claps and the players line up for a curtain call.

THE BACK YARD HAS NO LIMITS, it simply stretches out into the mulga. Each child has marked out the boundaries of its chosen territory, on which it proceeds to create a child-sized version of the world in which it lives. The older boy builds a tiny bough shed as a concession to a homestead and busily builds paddocks and a set of yards, perfect in detail down to the bronco panel. A plastic toy horse drags roped lizards up to the panel, where a pretence is made of branding and earmarking them. He track-rides his boundaries and sinks bores and puts up windmills in strategic places. Southern Cross, who provide the windmills for the stations of the adult world, send out several small demonstration mills, which take pride of place on the children's stations. The boy's friend, who has come to stay indefinitely, works his property in a similar vein, but taking his lead from the other more forceful child. Both of them employ the smallest boy to help with fencing and drilling, since he has decided that he does not want a station of his own. He feels the enormity of such an enterprise and prefers to be an itinerant among his propertied siblings. Perhaps he is already suspicious of the thrall which land exerts, an attitude he is to carry into adulthood.

The little girl puts much of her attention into the homestead, carefully built from a cardboard carton, with all the necessary rooms and a piece of tin for its roof. She plants a lawn and small twigs for trees, which she waters regularly, and has her small brother help her build a fence to keep the stock out. Many of the dramas of her world take place around the homestead, with its people, poddy calves and foals, dogs, cats, and chooks. Beyond it is a magical domain, in which anything is possible. She is a beautiful child with a determined nature, miscast in her position in the family as the third child out of four.

The smallest boy lives to a great extent in his own world, largely overlooked among more assertive and capable siblings. He spends a lot of his time in the Aboriginal camp, pottering about annoying the women, who tell him about the demons and spirits which inhabit the local landscape, in order to instil in him a proper fear and respect or to frighten him into going home to the safety of the big house.

He is a willing participant in the games devised by his blonde sister. These two live in the shadow of the older brother and sister, knowing they cannot hope to achieve the status of the Girl and the Boy. This disturbs the little girl more than her younger brother, who is happy enough to avoid the expectations attached to such status.

When the oldest sister comes home from boarding school for holidays, she is taken on a detailed tour of the stations, given a demonstration of lizard branding and bore drilling, shown the careful small fences and the dimensions of each property. She is so taken with them that for a moment she is tempted to join them, to mark out her own piece of country which will encompass the rough outcrops of limestone and bits of bare baked red sand. Her mind is busy with possibilities. But regretfully she gives up the idea. She is not part of their world any more.

The arrival at the station always takes her by surprise. Often they arrive towards nightfall, having left town the previous day and camped somewhere along the track. She is overwhelmed by the colours of the falling dusk, the beat of the generator that is such a small sound in the prevailing silence, the yellow light of the homestead verandah and the cheerful shouting of children. These arrivals are in their way almost as painful as the departures. All the closed vulnerable places in her are invaded by feelings which she can hardly bear.

The children dance along the verandah and claim her. She is clutched and pulled to come and look, see here. A white mouse with babies, a drawing of a rough-tail goanna stealing duck eggs, new puppies. And tomorrow we have to show you the new chickens, and the colts that are being broken in, and the poddy calves. The smallest brother is hovering, not big enough to make himself heard, about to be tearful. The girl reaches through a welter of arms and legs for him. She is home. It is real.

Away from it, it does not exist. It must be a place she has imagined, infiltrating between the louvre-banded light of classrooms. It is neverland, a dreamscape displaced by the scepticism of schoolgirls.

—Nobody lives out there!

And who is she, against all this female certainty, to hold out and say—I do. She is rendered homeless, the world circumscribed between dormitory and classroom walls. But here among children on the evening-lit verandah it is real, and she is home. The pain of having to leave it again is inseparable from the joy of being here.

At night, unable to sleep, she goes out into the darkness and begins to walk. There is a half-moon, bright enough to see clearly by, and she walks for a long time, away from the homestead, until she is on the track to the lake. About her she can sense many small movements of night creatures, and once a piece of the darkness takes the shape of a black dingo which crosses her path and becomes darkness again. She must touch everything as she passes, the hard earth of the anthills, the soft shredding bark of the ti-tree, the fine sandpapery texture of leaves of the desert gums, even thrusting a hand into a spiny clump of spinifex and pulling it back through the soft feathery seed heads. As she approaches the lake the sand becomes softer, and she kneels and then lies flat, face-down, hearing a heartbeat which must be her own drumming back into her head from the earth.

The lake is shallow, the moonlight makes the surface appear like a sheet of tin. The ti-tree throws bent and twisted shadows which make a mad black unmoving dance on the sand. At the edge of the water she takes off her clothes and wades out. It is like wading into a pool of mercury, heavy silver stuff which beads and runs from her thighs. In front of her the water is perfectly still, and she can see to the far shore. Behind her the ripples are sluggish, a slow drift of indigo channels back to the shelf of sand where she entered the water. At the centre of the lake the water is waist high, and she turns then and looks back, and spins about slowly until she has scanned the whole circle of the shoreline. The water is warm, and she crouches until she is kneeling in the mud on the bottom, and then dips further, beginning to pull up handfuls of the mud and plaster it on her breasts and face and belly. She smears herself in an ecstacy of mud, rolling about in the water, and stands mud-coated, sliced off at the navel.

SHE GOES DOWN IN THE MORNING to the yards, where they are breaking in the new colts. It involves sweat and dust and some blood, and a subdued but focused energy. To watch the horsebreaker in action is to see a process of attraction and seduction, the horse, once it overcomes its initial fear, as coy and tentative as a shy teenager. The girl watches from the steel rails of the round yard. The horsebreaker moves like a boxer, or a dancer, responsive always to the creature with which he is engaged in this fragile partnership. When the colt nudges the man and is rewarded with a palm sliding gently and firmly down the side of its head, she feels the same hand brush her face from brow to jaw, closing over nose and mouth in an inexorable, quiet grip. She watches the brown hands touch the colt and imagines them touching her.

When they do, some years later, it is exactly as she had expected. Like the colt she reels away, afraid of and desiring to be touched, and then comes back for more. Whether it is only horses that he understands, or girls, she couldn't say. He is gentle and infinitely patient. The most recalcitrant colt is won over in the end by his strange tenacious affection.

The horsebreaker is bound to this country by blood and knowledge. He belongs here, and only here. Through him she touches the country. Later, when she hears herself described as being 'broken in' by him, she can only concur. It doesn't matter, because by then she has long moved on, but she remembers him with affection. After all, he loved all his horses, and always treated them well.

10

TODAY I OFFERED TO DO a day's mustering because they are a man short in the stock camp. They are mustering around Wild Potato Bore, bringing the cattle back to the homestead. Wild Potato was the main camp. I know this country so well, though there is a fence line now from the camp to the bore. They have fenced in some of the plains country. The timber yards are ramshackle, the remains of the bough shed at the old camp are still standing. I have forgotten nothing, the daylight start, the sudden chill just before sunrise, the smell of saddle blankets and the recalcitrance of cold leather. I am already thinking I must be mad to do this voluntarily. I know exactly how it is going to feel. The skin rubbed raw on the legs, nose and mouth clogged with dust, the ache of unaccustomed muscles being called on.

The Aboriginal stockmen ride a little apart, bemused by my presence. I ride up and ask the oldest of them how long he has worked here. He has white hair and a young face, it is impossible to tell his age.

—Long time. I worked for Fred Colson, Peter Seidle, Joe Mahood.

He is abrupt, had saddled his horse with an off-handed flair, and is obviously a good horseman, though hard on the horse. I tell him I am Joe Mahood's daughter. He knows I know he never worked for my father.

One of the other stockmen, young and plump, asks me—You grew up here?

—Yes, with my brothers and sister.

He is curious about me. His name is Ronny Bumblebee, and this is traditional country for him.

In fact we don't muster but wait at the bore while the small plane which flew in last night brings the cattle in from the sandhills to the south. We wait a long time in the freezing wind, with bursts of dust lifting from time to time out on the flat. The windmill spins and creaks, and the water from the overflow pipe spins out in a silver ribbon. One of the horses is startled into shying and pigrooting, dislodging its rider. He makes no attempt to hang on and flaps to the ground like a bundle of rags. He huddles there, looking embarrassed, while the white-haired stockman gallops off after his horse. They are gone for some time, but eventually the horse trots back with the rider on its tail. Both stirrup leathers are gone, so there is a search until they are found. The young Aborigine reluctantly gets back on the horse. He is not happy. He is not a good rider, and there is a fair chance the horse will get the better of him again at some stage during the day.

He reminds me of a boy who came from the mission next door to do a mustering season. There is the same passivity and half-ashamed demeanour. The other stockmen tolerated him, it was not in their nature to victimise him. But they were mildly scornful of the young men from the mission, who didn't learn stock-camp skills, couldn't ride well and whose traditional culture had been largely supplanted by mission training. When they caught him stealing tobacco the other stockmen came to my father, for fear he would think it was them.

Cattle are beginning to trickle in over the sand dunes, and there is some activity in order to hold them at the bore. I'm grateful to be able to move and get a little warmer. The plane does a few more sweeps until it becomes clear there are no more cattle to come, and we start moving the mob along. We hold them at a dam a few kilometres away and stop for dinner camp, then start them up for the walk back to the homestead. Every clump of spinifex and anthill is familiar, I am no longer sure that twenty years have elapsed. The stockmen could easily be the stockmen I worked with as a teenager. The dust in my mouth and eyes is the same dust I tasted then, my irritation at being left at the tail of the mob is the same. The difference is that now I ride out onto the wing instead of staying in the dust and accepting my place at the bottom of the pecking order. Someone else can push the tail along for a while. The discomfort is the same, the sore legs at the beginning of the season, the cold, the dry skin, the hair and eyes full of dust. Most of the time I couldn't wait for it to be over. But I would never miss an opportunity to spend time in the stock camp and did a full season when I was seventeen. This was where the real life of the station existed for me.

SHE IS ALWAYS SECRETLY a little afraid for the first few days in the stock camp. Afraid of making some serious blunder, of being in the wrong place, of not knowing what to do. But she has made her choice. This is where one learns to act. This is where one chooses between acting and being acted upon. There has never been a question of where her alliances lie. She is, after all, her father's daughter. With the encroachment of puberty she has cropped her long hair and is frequently mistaken for a boy. She cannot separate her own desires from her father's expectations of her. She cannot tell where the boundary between them lies.

It is always taken for granted that she will choose to spend her school holidays in the camp. The stock work is a means of re-establishing her position as a competent and significant part of life on the station. And she does prefer it, on the whole, to the domestic routines of the homestead, a world of women and children, of which she is neither, though subtly pulled between the two. The women she knows are plump and passive, or raw-boned and strident, or her mother, who is too close for comfort. There is nothing in the stuff of their daily lives that she wants for herself. Their lives are built around the maintenance of family and homestead, teaching children, endless amounts of cooking and cleaning and washing. She does not grasp that there might be compensations and pleasure concealed somewhere in all this. It seems to her a world of relentless and inescapable drudgery.

She prefers her clearly defined difference in the world of the stock camp, a white girl among black men, simultaneously privileged as the boss's daughter and lowest on the pecking order for her lack of experience. The rules are clear, the prohibitions unassailable, the value of achieving a level of skill and competence unquestionable. She has chosen the pared-down simplicity of the swag and campfire, from which she often yearns after the comforts of the homestead, though she would never have admitted it.

This first day she goes out with the stockmen to kill a bullock. The last of the salt meat has been eaten, and everyone is hungry for fresh beef. Her father has insisted they use the 310 rifle, because with the 303 there is too much risk of killing the horsetailer or wounding the horse plant. The beast they choose is a big, quiet red bullock, and the plan is to drive up close and shoot him from the vehicle. Harry is driving, and Rex has the gun. As they drive towards the bullock the beast throws up his head, and Rex throws up the gun at the same time and fires, the way they do it in the movies. The bullet pings off somewhere harmlessly and there is a cackle of laughter from the front of the vehicle.

Big Mick, who is on the back with the girl, says with a grin—Rex can't shoot.

The bullock watches them, a little suspiciously, and the girl wills him to make a run for it.

Harry has the gun now and drives one-handed with the barrel resting on the window frame. He is a better shot than Rex and actually hits the bullock somewhere. The beast bellows with fright and surprise and gallops off with his tail in the air. The Toyota plunges after him across the spinifex, and Mick and the girl cling to the back as Harry blasts off a couple more shots, both of which hit the bullock but only make him run faster. Mick leans down and shouts to Harry in lingo, and Harry passes the gun up to him. The girl crouches down as low as she can get and wishes she does not have to witness what is going to happen next.

Harry wheels the Toyota past the fleeing bullock and blocks it, then Mick takes a shot at close range. He hits the beast in the eye, but it is not enough to bring the bullock down. He shoots again, another head shot, and the beast begins to run in circles, flinging his head from side to side as if to shake off the mutilated eye. Mick keeps shooting until the magazine is empty, but the animal keeps stumbling about, refusing to fall down. Mick shouts and the vehicle stops and he leaps off with the axe in his hand. At the same time Harry jumps out and grabs the bullock by the tail and pulls him down. Big Mick swings the axe, all sixteen stone of him behind the blunt-sided axeblow to the skull of the wounded beast. The animal stretches momentarily rigid before giving a long shudder, as if relieved to be finally dead. Rex is already there with the butcher knife, cutting deeply through the hide of the throat and into the jugular. He digs a channel for the blood, which pulses out in a bright pink froth. They stand around grinning. Mick mimes Rex with the gun, and they all break up with laughter. Harry says better they leave the gun next time and just bring Mick with the axe. Rex makes a fire, and as they cut up the animal they throw scraps of meat onto the flames, then eat them, barely singed. When they bring the meat back to the camp the horsetailer says laconically he thought someone must have started a war out there.

Some time in the night horses wake her, moving quietly away from the camp, hobbles clinking faintly, to be gone as far as possible before the horsetailer sets out to look for them before dawn. She wakes again to a shadow of movement as the horsetailer leaves the camp. He must have them back and yarded by daylight. The musterers will be on the move by sunrise.

From her swag the girl watches the horses come in. They make no sound save for an occasional clink of the hobbles strung around their necks. The sound of their hooves is muffled in the soft earth. They have come out of the night country, dark shapes against a sky which has barely begun to lighten. They have yet to take on the material substance of day creatures. The horsetailer rides bareback behind them, a shadow of a horseman driving shadows of horses.

Now there is movement at the campfire. She can see her father's silhouette, stoking the fire. The radio is on a country music station, crooning mournfully into the darkness. These mornings she is always out of the swag quickly, she could not bear to be thought slow or unwilling. It is cold, her boots are stiff and icy as she pulls them on, and she struggles into her short woollen coat. She has slept fully dressed and has a clean shirt and underwear under her pillow. The swag is basic, a sleeping bag, blanket and pillow. It is not too difficult to leave it.

They are moving camp today, to the next bore. Her father will take the stock-camp trailer and set up camp, and several of the stockmen will drive the sale mob. This has cut down the musterers to five. They ride out together for the first hour, and cut some fresh tracks over the first sandridge. The riders split, two to follow the tracks, three to make a wider sweep. The girl rides out with Harry and Rex. They don't talk much. There is a slight constraint between them, although the stockmen have known her since she was a child. They are all used to it and manage it well enough. There has always been a mutual regard between them, never spoken. Their grins of approval mean a great deal to her. To read a track, bring back a beast, throw a rope, and win that brief white flash of teeth in a black face will remain for her a sheerer measure of worth than anything she is to encounter in later life. From time to time she asks them the name of something in their language. She is trying to learn the hybrid lingo used on the station—Wolmajarri with a sprinkling of Warlpiri and Kukatja—but is hampered by self-consciousness.

They ride suddenly onto the skeleton of a mare and foal. The foal is half born, head and forefeet through the mare's pelvis, the rest of the tiny bones trapped in the cage of her body. It is a parable in bone, laid out on a patch of open red ground, untouched by dingoes. There is not much to mark a struggle. The mare seems to have died quietly enough, exhausted no doubt from the exertions of the labour. The foal would barely have glimpsed life before it died. The riders look down on it from a great height, arbitrary witnesses surprised by a cage of bone arching out of the sparse clumps of dry grass.

Riding back in the late afternoon behind the cattle they have flushed out of the dunes, Rex carries a newborn calf across the withers of his horse. The girl feels her body dissolve into the light, her self moving upwards and outwards until it is nothing but air and light.

All night the cattle sing and mumble in the unaccustomed constraints of the cable and timber yards. The girl falls asleep to the thin wail of a dingo, remote beyond the murmuring cattle. Above her the sky tilts slowly towards morning as she wakes and sleeps and wakes again to the small soft movements of the waking camp.

By daylight the branding fire is lit, the brands lined up and beginning to heat, and the bronco horse is in harness. He is new to the job, just learning, a big solid amiable young horse with Percheron blood. Harry uncoils the rope from the heavy saddle, loops it out and over the head of a calf, which leaps and flings itself bellowing at full stretch away from the rope. The horse leans imperturbably against the calf's weight, dragging it up to the timber bronco panel, and the stockmen rope a fore and hind leg, tying them off to the ends of the panel. It is a male calf, and Scotty, the smallest stockman, grabs the free hind leg, hauling it out straight and exposing the small testicles, which her father excises neatly from the scrotal sac with a sharp pocket knife. The girl runs with the brand. There is the quick stink of burning hair as she plants it on the woolly rump and returns it to the fire. The head rope is pulled off and a shape nipped neat as a piece of jigsaw puzzle from the bottom of the ear. As the leg ropes are removed the calf leaps to its feet and gallops, yelling, to the middle of the mob. Its mother searches aggressively, butting away strange calves and calling an answer to her howling child. The whole process has taken less than a minute, and already Harry has a second calf on the rope, a heifer this time. Mick searches in the dust for the discarded testicles and places them carefully in a billycan, a delicacy for later.

By midmorning they have branded a hundred and fifty calves, and Mick's billycan is overflowing. The girl is flushed and sweating from the fire and has been thinking about the smoko break for some time now. They are into the tail end of the cleanskins, some big mickeys which escaped last year's branding. Rex has brought in the old bronco horse, who does not wear himself out against the bigger animals but simply stands his ground and then moves when the rope slackens. A mickey lashes out at the leg rope and catches her father unexpectedly in the midriff, dropping him instantly unconscious to the ground. He looks suddenly small and fragile, his shirt a stain of blue on the red earth, and the girl drops the brand and runs to his side. The stockmen leg-rope the mickey and tie him down, then stand back from the fallen man, who comes to and props himself up, laughing shakily into his daughter's stricken face. The offending mickey lies utterly passive against the bronco panel and is summarily castrated, earmarked, branded and released. It seems an appropriate moment to stop for smoko. As they walk to the camp low murmurs of laughter break from the black stockmen. Because it is the boss who was kicked, it is not an occasion for the kind of hilarity it would have caused had it been one of them, but already they are making a story of it for the evening campfire.

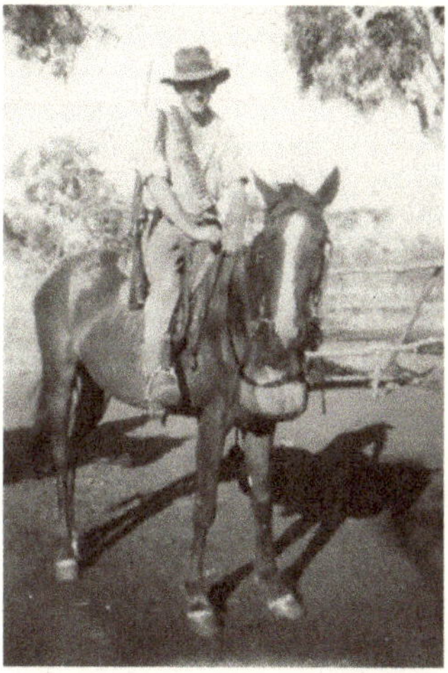

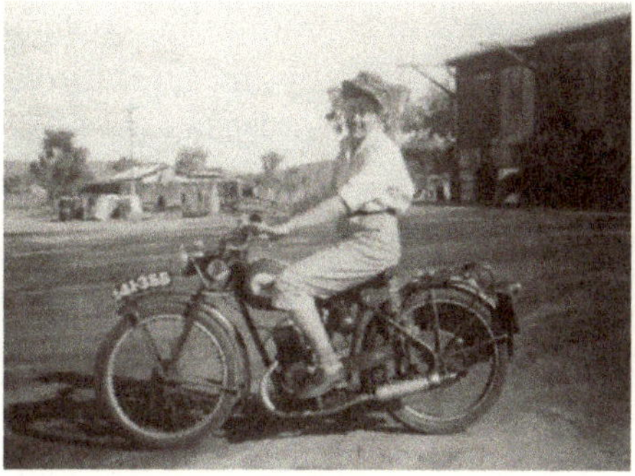

11

Back at the homestead I try to record in my journal some of the sensations and emotions this return has provoked. I sit in the green vinyl armchair and hunt through the pages of my father's station diary for something that will anchor me to this place that is so unchanged, so utterly changed.

The diary begins on Sunday, October 6th, 1963, written in fountain pen in my father's beautiful handwriting. It is mostly a log of activities, of sinking and equipping bores, of track-riding and trucking stock, of checking waters and getting the homestead established. What emerges is a daily tracery of movement about the country, a constant struggle with broken-down vehicles and bores and equipment, of stock perishing and of men pulling out. The ubiquitous killer, the term used for the beast killed for meat, is mentioned about every six or seven days, beef providing the staple diet. I find the first entry for today's date, 21st June.

Sunday, 21st June, 1964
South of Ferdie's through the sand ridges to Skeleton Valley.

Should be easy for water.
Looked at several places across to W. boundary.
Back to Lake Alec. Camped.
Warm day. No wind.

My father described Skeleton Valley to me, but I never saw it. It was an ancient watercourse of eroded limestone, a lost valley carved into the forms of mythical beasts and skulls and headstones. It was drilled successfully and good water was found at a site nearby, which was named the Graveyards. Windmill parts ferried in through the dunes were discovered to belong to two different mills which did not fit together (at least this is the story I have from hearsay). Other priorities took precedence, and the job of equipping the Graveyards bore became one of those chores to be dealt with when time allowed. According to Adam, who has flown over the site, the windmill parts are still clearly visible from the air. He tried to reach the site once, following invisible hints of an old track, but ran out of spare tyres and turned back. On the map he has given me the bore is wrongly marked as salty. I find myself obscurely pleased to know that the Graveyards and Skeleton Valley remain inaccessible, an unresolved fragment from my father's story.

June 21st, 1965 and 1966 are recorded in the diary, but there are no entries for either day. Weeks of days and dates are neatly inscribed, as if insisting upon the formal passage of time. A uniform number of lines are left between the dates, allocating each day an equal value. Among the pages of the unwritten diary I hear a whisper of my father's other voice. But it is too soon. I am not ready to listen yet.

Instead I flick back through the brief entries which reiterate vehicle and windmill breakdowns, staff and stock movements, more breakdowns, occasional visits to hospital with injuries.

My father's personality remains almost invisible in the written word, though a rare dry remark hints at irony. There is no evidence of the streak of self-parody which emerged when he played the guitar, warbling his way mournfully through 'China Doll' and 'High Noon'. He had a good singing voice, and he made up in panache whatever his guitar-playing lacked in finesse. The guitar was put away when he stopped drinking, and he did not play again for years. He was a good storyteller, and something of a ham actor and mimic, leaping to his feet and gesturing extravagantly to illustrate the dramatic moments of an anecdote. His sense of humour was acute but unreliable, for he only sometimes took himself lightly. When he felt his dignity infringed on he would retreat, leaving a large oppressive absence which we skirted guiltily.

The diary gives none of this away. My father moves through the pages, a small, broad-shouldered man. He did not have the strut I remember as characteristic of many men of his stature. In fact he never seemed small, for he carried about with him a sense of natural authority, compounded by the hint of something hidden, potentially dangerous. The danger was psychological, not physical. He was not a violent man, though capable of immense reserves of physical energy when required. And the danger, one felt, was mostly to himself.

The entry for May 19th, 1964 triggers a sharp snapshot of memory.

> Worked on tractor. Did stock take.
> Tried grader out. Bill W, Ferdie, Bob S arrived.
> Ferdie's offsider bushed on bike. Found him and brought bike back.
> Bob hit offsider. Bill hit Bob. Good evening was had by all.
> Definitely a dry camp.

'A dry camp' is the colloquial term for a place where alcohol is banned. My father did not follow through with his intention on this occasion, and it was some years later, when my father gave up drinking himself, before the station was declared dry.

It is impossible to talk about men in the Outback without talking about alcohol. I was in my twenties before I realised that drinking could be a civilised and moderate activity. My experience of drinking was of a process in which the men became progressively cheerful, aggressive, maudlin and violent, while the women, with a few exceptions, became cheerful, angry, aggrieved and frightened. There was usually a point where the women and children cleared out, either to go home, to take refuge with someone or simply to hide out in the darkness, out of range of the stumbling violence beginning to erupt among the men.

The episode described in my father's diary happened before the family moved to the station. My mother drove out during the school holidays with the older of my brothers and I. It was her first visit, and mine. The camp was a large bough shed, with an open campfire protected by a corrugated iron windbreak, and a rough timber bench for cooking. Dangerous Dan the drilling contractor was in residence, with his wife and a young child. We had been there for a few days when the visitors arrived. The drinking must have started in the afternoon. At some point Ferdie's young offsider, who was from Adelaide, took the motorbike for a ride. After some time it became evident that he was either lost or had had an accident. The men tracked him down easily enough and found him weeping and hysterical as darkness was beginning to fall. He had become disoriented and panicked, unable to follow his own tracks back to the road. He was hit, I think, because he was weeping and afraid.

Bill hit Bob presumably because Bob hit the boy. I know everyone hit someone because they were drunk. I remember the darkness closing in around something fractured, an outrage on the brink of grief. The men's voices were husky and congested with drunkenness and anger. The children and the women pulled back, out of range. Isolated between them was the young man from Adelaide, whom I remember only as a shape sobbing in the dusk.

THERE WERE MEN SCATTERED all through the country whose lives seemed forever on the verge of being overtaken by fate. Their business partners disappeared with the chequebook, their wages didn't get paid, often there was a woman lurking in the background in a dangerous and unpredictable state. They seemed always to be injuring themselves. Bits of windmills fell on them, horses kicked them, bad food and too much rum poisoned them, minor extremities were torn off by ropes and machinery. They lost their swags and their dogs and their jobs. They got stranded in Queensland with no money and broken-down cars and pregnant girlfriends. They walked into brawls without looking and got charged with disturbing the peace. They got picked up by girls when they went to town and found themselves in compromising situations with fifteen year olds. Their lives ran along an edge that threatened constantly to cut them to pieces. They seemed unbearably foolish and fragile, and my child's heart suffered torment that they seemed always in such danger.

But they were full of humour and panache. There was a sheer exuberant physicality about them that was about being male and young. Broken collarbones and broken ribs didn't stop them pulling down a recalcitrant steer or riding a rough horse. They picked themselves up laughing out of the dirt. Physical courage was a given. What their inner lives consisted of, I have no notion. The articulate among them described their adventures more often than not with self-deprecating humour. The best stories were usually the ones of which they were the butt. The inarticulate had stories told about them and sometimes came off the better for it, since it was acceptable to eulogise the style and skill of others.

There wasn't much mercy extended to the foolish or the incompetent. Ironic nicknames stuck. If someone was referred to as the Ringer it usually meant he wasn't. The Kiwi Ringer was passing through from somewhere to anywhere and needed a job. He rode very badly, to the huge entertainment of the Aboriginal stockmen, particularly Scotty. Scotty was small and strong, with a head of matted fair ringlets, and he rode a big hammer-headed wall-eyed horse called Woolly. Scotty laughed so hard at the sight of the Kiwi Ringer bouncing around in the saddle that he nearly fell off his own horse, setting off the other stockmen. He kept his head turned away out of politeness, but the shrieks and cackles bubbled out of him every time he rolled his eyes back at the stubby, uncomfortable figure.

Things didn't improve for the Kiwi Ringer. He proved to be lethargic and slow-witted, lying about the camp reading Deadwood Dicks when the team was not mustering. The head stockman Malley, the most good-natured and amiable of men, was exasperated to the point of shoving him around the fire on a particularly slow-moving morning. When the Ringer learned that he was on the same wage as the

Aboriginal stockmen, he was affronted and demanded a raise. My father, initially speechless, told the Ringer that he, the Ringer, should be paying him, the boss, for putting up with him. The Ringer gave notice and then hung disconsolately about the camp for a week before he could cadge a lift back to town with the mission truck.

Another ringer inhabits the early pages of the station diary. There is no explanation of how he came by his name, but the cryptic diary entries chart his brief career as an employee.

> 28th October 1963—Gave the Mad Ringer and G. Dann jobs.
> 15th November—Ringer handling the mob and doing a good job. Advised him he could have station job when he finishes with mob.
> 25th Nov—Ringer arrived about 3.00 pm, so gave him rest of day to spell. He can now take over job as general handyman around the station.
> 26th Nov—Ringer getting the place very tidy and shipshape.
> 13th Dec—Sent Ringer into town with Blitz to take boy to hospital.
> 14th Dec—Ringer got back late night.
> 16th Dec—Found out that Ringer took 4 pigs and an unauthorised trip to Moyles. Also found out Ringer did not deliver the mail to Moyles.
> 17th Dec—Dismissed Ringer.

A pair of contractors earn the names Hydraulic and Trewalla, on the grounds that 'what one couldn't lift the other one would'. This does not refer to their physical strength but to their propensity for thieving. The stock-route bore they were contracted to equip, and which they named Sangster's Well after the girlfriend of one of them, was renamed Gangster's when my father discovered a cache of stolen tools and equipment stashed in a hole hollowed out of the side of the well.

Men found their way to the Outback for all sorts of reasons. There were dreamers, like my father. There were misfits and misogynists and escapists and eccentrics and criminals. Some were on the run from wives or the law, some were looking for an opportunity to live out a fantasy. Most of them came north looking for a place where the constraints of society were more elastic, where they could be themselves, or leave behind the selves that had accumulated too much uncomfortable baggage.

My father was essentially a rather shy man. He was thoughtful, sensitive and somewhat introverted. He was a contradiction in the tough and macho world of the Outback, but when I look back there is hardly a man I can think of who fulfilled the stereotype. They looked the part, lean and sun-browned and sinewy, but the sense I have of most of them is of their vulnerability, their weaknesses, their unsuccessful attempts to conceal their inadequacies. So much of the work they did involved mending things that got broken. Vehicles, windmills, welders, generators, fences, troughs. They spent their time grappling with the recalcitrance of machinery and weather and the sheer intransigence of the country itself. It was a kind of heroism, not of the grand gesture but of mundane perseverance.

My memory presents the men as much more fragile than the women. Yet it is the men's lives that attracted me, their lives that lent validity to the Outback myth with which I identified.

FERDIE WAS A HANDSOME Austrian with a luminous smile, as long as he kept his mouth closed. When he opened it his teeth were green and terrible, for he never cleaned them. He ate things which would have destroyed a lesser constitution, and neutralised the dangerous bacteria with overproof rum. A policeman on bush patrol who called at his camp and was offered a meal was confronted with the remains of a partly skinned dingo. When Ferdie applied for a gun licence on the grounds that he shot his own food, the young policeman confirmed the veracity of this claim.

Ferdie's profession was drilling for water, and although he was under thirty he had a reputation for living hard and running a tough camp. He came to the Territory at the age of ten, on foot, with his older brother and sister. To these immigrant children some sort of magic must have resonated in the name of Alice Springs, for they abandoned their parents, who had recently settled unhappily in Adelaide, and set off along the railway line, following the route of the Afghan camel traders through the desert. They begged and stole from the fettlers' camps along the line, cadged lifts, told lies and no doubt had some strange and dangerous encounters. There were some hard-bitten characters among the fettlers, for it was a place where no questions were asked and anonymity was a given. It was common enough for a man to walk away from the railway line and his fellow workers into the great blank of the desert, leaving behind him only an alias and a half-empty bottle of rum. It must have surprised even the fettlers to see a trio of children with hardly a word of English between them materialise out of the mirage into their camps.

The children duly reached Alice, where they hid in a warehouse until they were discovered by some local residents and fostered by several families until they were old enough to take care of themselves. Somewhere along the way Ferdie acquired his softly accented English, a partnership in a drilling rig and an affinity with the remote, secretive contours of the country. He spent months alone in it, learning the lie of the land, developing an intuition for the pockets and declivities where water seeped and stayed. He had a dog called Maxie, a lean pink-spotted mutt who had the habit of snapping at the branches of mulga trees from the back of Ferdie's ute. Often he was left hanging by his clamped jaws from an overhanging branch, the ute speeding on ahead of its banner of red dust. Maxie finally perished while following a small plane which was flying Ferdie into Alice Springs. Somewhere out in the desert the dog gave up, having gone too far to turn back.

Ferdie was not always alone by choice. His reputation for hard rations and harder work made it difficult to get offsiders, and he was known to have picked up the odd hitchhiker on the way out of town and lied about his real destination. When they reached his camp the traveller's choice was to stay and work for a month or so, or find his own way out. Relief at discovering he had merely been shanghaied, and was not in the clutches of a maniac or murderer, generally made the hitchhiker philosophical, and no doubt he dined out on the story for years afterwards.

There was a time when Ferdie called on my mother to rescue him from the clutches of a lady known to the town as 'the Black Widow', a reference to the effect she had on the men in her life. Ferdie was neither intelligent nor intuitive about women. But some instinct for self-preservation told him to remove himself from the web of the Widow. He enlisted my mother and us to pose as his wife and family. We hammed it up dreadfully, and I doubt the unfortunate woman was fooled. I remember her, thin and dark and haunted-looking; she took in at a glance the shiny cheerful self-satisfied facade we presented and was defeated without a fight.

Ferdie epitomised a type of immigrant Australian who discovered in the inland a place where it was possible to abandon all but the basic constraints of society. He was less eccentric than some, who lived in overturned water tanks on the edge of remote towns, or in burrows on the opal fields, or disappeared into the North Queensland rainforest to live like Tarzan. But his life was of a kind with theirs, as if the vast historic weight of European culture was sloughed off on that first encounter with the light and space of the desert, and the makeshift substitute culture he encountered was rendered almost invisible against the hard clarity of landscape.

RAY REFERRED TO HIMSELF as the green-eyed blackfellow. He was tall and dark-skinned, though in that environment of multiple skin shades he was a long way short of black. He was a member of one of those extended Central Australian families whose heritage crosses most of the available racial boundaries. He had aunts and uncles and cousins who might boast in one direction links with European aristocracy or, in another, a geneology which entitled them to forty thousand years or more of ancestral links to the surrounding country. The slanting eyes of one relative might conjure a Chinese gold prospector, the high-bridged nose and profile of another suggest the legacy of Afghan camel drivers. Ray could easily have carried the blood of camel drivers, for he was tall and hawk-profiled, and his green eyes were remarkable. But as far as he knew he was the standard Centralian cross, white man, Aboriginal woman, and he wore his mixed heritage like a crown of thorns, though cocked always at a rakish angle. Sober, he sent himself up. Drunk, he picked fights. He was tall and lean and tough, but he picked his fights with the biggest, meanest, toughest white men. They enraged him because they were white and he wasn't, and he flung his Aboriginality in their faces and challenged them to abuse it, which they did. He had been beaten up at one time or another by most of the reputed fighters in the Centre, and the stories of his fights made good telling in his sober rueful phases.

Ray came back from the Halls Creek races one year with a black eye and a broken nose. This time he had refused to move his swag from the middle of the road, on the grounds that there were too many bindi-eyes everywhere else. The perpetrator of the damage was a truckie who wanted to drive his vehicle along that particular stretch of the road.

—It was the middle of the night. I told him to piss off. When he got out of the truck he was built like a brick shithouse. I never even had time to get out of the swag.

To add insult to injury he had to spend hours picking the bindi-eyes out of his groundsheet.

From time to time he would go north to Darwin and hang out with the local hippies on one of the beaches, getting stoned and telling lies. He would bring a whole lot of new stories back for us, of his adventures among the misfits and eccentrics of the tropics. Stories were Ray's currency. He made us laugh. One day he didn't come back from the north, and we heard he had gone to sleep on the railway line and lost both his legs. We never saw him again.

THE NIGHT OUTSIDE IS LISTENING. I remember this listening stillness. I listen with it, as I used to do, but all I hear is the confused chatter of my own thoughts. It is so strange to be here. This place has occupied a disproportionate space in my life, and I do not really understand why. Doris Lessing says in *African Laughter*—Every writer has a myth country. This does not have to be childhood. Myth does not have to be something untrue, but a distillation of truth.

This is my myth country. There is another quote, this time from Calvino, scrawled in my artist's notebook.

The storyteller of the tribe puts together phrases and images: the younger son gets lost in the forest, he sees a light in the distance, he walks and walks; the fable unwinds from sentence to sentence, and where is it leading? To the point at which something not yet said, something as yet only darkly felt by presentiment, suddenly appears and seizes us and tears us to pieces, like the fangs of a man-eating witch. Through the forest of fairy tale the vibrancy of myth passes like a shudder of wind.

Tonight, out here, that unseen shudder passes through the leaves of the mulga trees. Journeys are a kind of mythmaking. The myths of other places can't sustain me, but the cool inhuman wind shakes my fortitude.

PARTICIPATING IN MYTH demands a price, particularly the myth of failure which is so deeply embedded in this country. There is a term which resonates from my childhood, because I heard it first when I was of an age to visualise words literally.

—He's a bit of a no-hoper.
—That old no-hoper feller that lives with the blacks.
—The miserable bloody no-hoper!

I tried to imagine how it would be to have no hope, to be no hope. In my child's eye they looked like the lepers in my illustrated Bible, trailing banners of filthy rags, toothless and covered in weeping sores. My first real no-hoper was something of a disappointment. He was a nondescript fellow with scorched-looking skin and sandy hair. He did have bad teeth. But he was marked, set apart, as I had expected him to be. The place inside him where hope belonged was empty, that was quite clear. It was as if there was a vacuum, an absence at the heart of the country which made itself felt in men like him.

No-hopers were men. It was never used to describe women. I saw some of the laughing young men slide slowly across the boundary from irresponsible good nature to no-hoperdom. Black or white, alcohol was invariably a component. But the Aboriginal no-hoper was named by white society, measured by his lack of reliability and his loss of self-regard. The term as far as I can establish doesn't translate. He was generally cushioned by a system of kinship obligations which would never cast him out in the way a white no-hoper is cast out. In fact it wasn't uncommon for the white no-hoper to throw in his lot with the Aborigines, who treated him with tolerant scorn.

I once knew the son of a man who was a Territory legend. The old man, the father, was a wild and terrible character who was a law unto himself and had been responsible for the deaths of a number of Aborigines in his time. He had killed his first blackfellow when he was fourteen, by accident, shooting at him to liven him up and put a scare into him. In order to get rid of the evidence of his crime, for he and the Aborigine were alone with a mob of horses in the remote northern tableland country, the boy tried to burn the body on the campfire. As he sat in the darkness with God knows what thoughts going through his mind and the corpse slowly roasting on the campfire, he was treated to an apparition that stayed with him all his life. Up out of the flames came the body, sitting up with its scorching hair and its eye sockets pools of flame and the bones of its skull showing through the charred strips of its face. It was caused no doubt by the heat contracting the muscle and sinews, but the boy thought the dead blackfellow was coming out of the flames to wreak vengeance on him, and bolted howling into the night.

When he crept back to the fire he found the body fallen on its side and rendered harmless, and the next time he shot an Aborigine it was not by accident, and he did not try to burn the body. He took off one of his spurs and scratched a mark on the metal rail of the stockyards, and looked the other Aboriginal stockmen in the eye, shook his head and said— Poor bugger, killed by ricochet, you can see where the bullet bounced off the rail.

The son was a mere shadow of his father. He was tall and dark and handsome and hopeless. He played the guitar and danced well and told a good story. He was neither violent nor angry, and hadn't the stomach for shooting Aborigines, though he once shot a rooster in the main street of Borroloola in the early hours of the morning. It woke him up, he told the magistrate who fined him a thousand dollars, morning after morning at about three o'clock, until he could stand it no longer.

He was married long enough to father two children to a voluptuous redhead, before she left him and went home to her parents, taking the children with her. She took the children away because he drank, and he drank because she took his children away. He fell hopelessly in love with a woman who said she would leave him unless he stopped drinking. But he couldn't see the harm in it, since he never saw himself slobbering and unconscious, falling over people at social gatherings. He didn't take her seriously, and when she went he was dumbfounded. He drank himself into a stupor to drown his sorrows.

Later he pulled himself together and made a patched-up sort of life for himself. He drove trucks for a living, and from time to time there was talk of a partnership in a business, of buying his own truck, of acquiring a bit of land. But somehow the schemes never quite materialised, and one day he was in his early fifties, still drinking and still not over the woman who had left him twenty years before. And not too long after that he was found kneeling on the steps of his trailer home, after a night of heavy drinking, choked to death on his own vomit.

Since I have grown up and lived in towns and cities I have seen a great many men like this. I have seen the equivalent in women, and in the young. So it is not the country which produces such people, but something within human society. The difference I found when I was growing up was that these men came into my life, they were a part of it. They could not be overlooked and forgotten. They were always there, a source of frustration, grief and irritation, rubbing your face in their plight. You were forced to understand that while there was nothing you could do to change them or their lives, you were nevertheless implicated in their condition.

12

TOMORROW A BIG WOMEN'S business ceremony begins near Billiluna Station, across the border in Western Australia. I have been in touch with the Balgo women's project officer to see if it is all right for me to attend. All the Aboriginal women from Tanami Downs have gone already. This morning an old man came over to ask me if I was going to the 'bijnis', and I told him yes. I will come back here when it is over. For the moment it is a relief to get back on the road, to slip back into the panacea of movement.

There are a couple of abandoned cars along the track to the border, and a scattering of beer cans, evidence that this is the grog run from Balgo to Rabbit Flat. I can almost hear my father's ashes rattling irritably in their India tea caddy. To leave rubbish behind on the track or at a campsite was a hanging offence in my childhood. I remember occasions when my father stalked into geological survey camps and demanded of a discomfited survey boss that he send whoever was responsible back to clean up the evidence of transient campsites.

The country shows the mark of the dry times. The cattle are lean, the land brittle and dusty. The perennial grass plains,

Davidson's 'very good pastoral country', are chewed to a yellow stubble. There are gates and fence lines, stock tanks and holding yards. The great empty wilderness of my memory is subdued, domesticated. I cannot help but feel regret.

Another measure of the changes, ironically, is this women's business for which I am heading. I cannot imagine such an event in the years when I lived in this country. Then, the notion that Aboriginal women had any sort of power would have been an absurdity. Now I am travelling towards an occasion which has been made possible through government funding and the involvement of white women co-ordinators (city girls for the most part, drawn by dreams and political ideals). It is an acknowledgement of the importance of the black women's relationship to their country. Philosophically I am excited by it, curious and hopeful. Closer to home I feel like a creature that evolved in a different time, stepping hesitantly into an unknown present.

THERE ARE NO WOMEN IN the Davidson journal, and none in my father's stock-route report. There are very few in the station diary. The domestic events of the homestead do not warrant mentioning unless there is some sort of drama, such as the homestead being threatened by bushfire. The women's names which recur on page after page are place names, lakes and springs and hills named after mothers and wives and daughters.

In 1900, in Davidson's era, the north was a man's country. But there were exceptions. In 1902 Daisy Bates made a droving trip with her husband and son. In her written account of the trip she refers to her husband only once, and then simply as the boss drover. In fact she mentions the

Chinese cook, who emerges as a distinct personality, far more frequently and familiarly than she mentions her husband. She talks about *her* cattle, *her* land, *her* plant of horses and men. She also apparently abandons the entire outfit, including husband and son, as soon as they reach their destination, and returns to Fremantle, after which she embarks on the work among the Aborigines for which she achieved her somewhat controversial fame. One feels a flicker of sympathy for the silent Jack Bates, whom Daisy apparently married with little regard for the fact that she was still married to Breaker Morant. Neither man seems to have pursued her with pleas or demands that she come back and be a proper wife and mother. Daisy struck an early blow for women to travel on their own terms in the bush, and to marry and leave whom they please, but she achieved it through a capacity to invent and reinvent herself which appears almost pathological. She also began a tradition which has steadily gained momentum, that of white women aligning themselves with Aboriginal people as a means of freeing themselves from the conventions of their own society.

We had our own local example, as cranky and complex a character as Daisy herself. The eccentric and eccentrically-named Olive Pink camped at Thompson's Rockhole near the Granites for several years in the 1940s, at a time when the population of the Tanami–Granites region consisted of three white miners and a small group of Aborigines. Having waged an increasingly vitriolic campaign against various government departments for their neglect of Aboriginal, particularly female Aboriginal, welfare, she moved to the Granites as an act of solidarity with the people whose rights she championed. Eventually she became too ill to remain and retreated to Alice Springs where she grew into the figure of legend I encountered as a child.

There is a revealing early letter, written while she was studying anthropology under AP Elkin, in which Miss Pink outlines her resistance to investigating only Aboriginal women.

> It would be no use talking to the women about the things Dr Elkin wants me to investigate . . . As you know, I am not fond of the company of my own sex for long. (I told you that in relation to whites & it's the same with blacks. I like talking about 'things'—ideas—& beliefs—(not food & babies & ornaments & love affairs & all the things a really womanly woman should! . . .
>
> I keep impressing on Mick & the others that white women know all the things white men know . . .
>
> I show them things in Spencer for the very reason you suggest not to!!!! To show that I know things black women may not know, so they may as well tell me others!

Miss Pink was the town witch during my childhood, the demoness around whom all sorts of apocryphal tales were woven. She would march down the street in her pith helmet and sandshoes, haranguing everyone she encountered. She lived in a hut on the tract of land which has since become her memorial, the Olive Pink Flora and Fauna Reserve, and it was a dare among the local children to sneak as close as possible to the hut and throw stones at it. Miss Pink would erupt from inside, looking like a deranged Victorian governess, brandishing a rifle and occasionally firing off shots and shouting threats. Like other children of my age in Alice Springs, I knew the stories about Miss Pink. I always kept carefully outside the boundaries of her territory, Miss Pink's Hill as we called it, for I had heard the tales of Miss Pink and her rifle. I knew the stories of her long-running battle with the firemen, whom she accused of unseemly dress (or lack of it), which resulted in her being evicted from her hut in Todd Street. I knew of her letters of complaint about the local aero club, who she claimed were in the habit of gliding low over her roofless corrugated-iron bathroom while she was in the tub. I knew, vaguely, that she had lived out bush with the Aborigines for a time. I knew she was a mad old woman obsessed with things sexual, Aboriginal and conservational. She was an example of what became of women who did not get married and who lived alone and who were full of unpopular and strongly held opinions.

I met her from time to time, in the local library or marching along in the sandy creek bed on her way to town. She was, on these occasions, surprisingly ordinary, though peculiarly dressed. She wore the pith helmet of legend, but my memory of her is in a belted cream gabardine raincoat. She was always pleasant and cheerful, though I remember her taking the librarian to task over some 'tripe' among the books she was returning. I watched her furtively from behind the safety of the library shelves, terrified that she might suddenly demand of me some embarrassing, self-revealing behaviour. This was someone who did not recognise the boundaries between what was acceptable behaviour and what was not. A brush with her might result in one suddenly finding oneself on the wrong side of the boundary, aligned with her in eccentric isolation.

I can imagine the figure she cut, in the 1930s and 40s, among the laconic bushmen and the outlaws and ruffians on the goldfields around the Granites. She must have been an extraordinarily strong-willed and remarkable woman, but she would have seemed to them merely absurd. Her middle-aged Victorian virginity, coupled with her outspoken attacks on the sexual behaviour of white men towards Aboriginal women, made her vulnerable to the kind of prurient scorn that bluestocking attitudes have always aroused.

She held opinions that put her beyond the pale, and her abrasive and difficult personality alienated most of the support for her pioneering research into Aboriginal culture. It is only now, since she is safely dead and cannot contradict the process of softening the rougher edges of her opinions, that her anthropological writings and her stance on land rights are being re-examined seriously. For a time, sobered by the example of Miss Pink and Daisy Bates, I wondered whether the only women who could exist on their own terms in the country were the eccentric and the mad, whether the resistance and difficulties they encountered made them madder and more eccentric. But maybe it was the other way around. Maybe the Outback allowed room for a personality like Miss Pink's to expand in all its cranky formidable visionary uniqueness. She pushed a little wider the gap opened by Daisy Bates, into which white women have continued to infiltrate in growing numbers.

When I was a child this process had barely begun. There were a few female anthropologists scattered about, but the notion of women's law as a separate and significant category in the understanding of Aboriginal society had not seeped through into the wider consciousness. Aboriginal women were visible enough, because of their role in the domestic life of homesteads, but behind them trailed something invisible, impenetrable, unknowable. They came into the homestead in their crisp clean dresses and washed dishes and swept floors and laughed and told stories. They went walking with the white children and taught them to read tracks and identify bush tucker and catch goannas. And then they went away into their own camps and houses and closed the doors, both metaphoric and actual. My only attempt to open one of these doors, a real one, resulted in having a boot thrown at me. I had gone after dark to deliver a message to the head stockman's wife, Daisy. The wife of the only other married stockman was staying with her, and I could hear their voices talking softly inside the main room of the house. I knocked and called out, and the voices stopped. I tried the door, pushed it partly open, and something hit it with a loud clunk. I yelled, there was a burst of nervous laughter, and Daisy embarrassedly let me in. They had thought I was one of the local devils which inhabit the night-time, coming to get them. Both women were out of their own country, huddled together each night for mutual support in a place full of wandering spirits.

Daisy was a quiet, introverted girl who did not much like white people. She never volunteered anything, worked quietly in the house and went away into her private world. So it was a surprise to us when telegrams began arriving from the Alice Springs police, asking after her whereabouts. Whatever she had done, we conjectured that it couldn't have been too bad, and replied to the telegrams that she had gone to Western Australia, whereabouts unknown. One morning my brother Bob spotted a police vehicle at the top gate. Daisy, washing dishes at the sink, looked stricken. The children grabbed her arm, dragged her out the front door and disappeared into the mulga as the policeman came up the back path from the shed. My mother and I gave him a cup of tea, made conversation, told him we had heard nothing of Daisy for months. When he had gone and I whistled the all-clear, we extracted the story of Daisy's brush with the law. She was in town, bored and miserable, awaiting the birth of her first child. Half a bottle of cream sherry activated her dislike of white people in general and policemen in particular. It wasn't too difficult to find a policeman to insult, hit, and escape from, in spite of being eight and a half months pregnant. I suspect it was the indignity of being assaulted and then outrun by a young woman so obviously pregnant that had kept the police on Daisy's trail for so long.

Millie came to us before Daisy. She had known my mother years before, in another part of the country. Millie was outgoing, cheerful, articulate, almost a stereotype of the fat, jolly, motherly black woman. She had a pierced nasal septum, through which she used to stick matches with a great sleight-of-hand flourish to amuse us. With Millie we went tracking and digging. She told us stories and painted our faces. Fat as she was, no goanna could outrun her. When one of the stockmen came to my father in a state of great embarrassment to tell him he had contracted gonorrhoea from her, my father was furious, especially since it fell to him to administer her medication. He was a prudish man. He did not want to have to deal with the messy evidence of clandestine sexual activity. Millie treated the matter with equanimity. When my father arrived at her shed with the first of the daily penicillin injections, intending to administer it in her arm, she presented him with a large bare rump. He admitted later that it tickled his sense of the absurd, that he of all people should find himself in such a situation.

AT WILSON'S CAVE, THE LAST bore on the Tanami Downs side of the Western Australian border, I stop and boil the billy. It is not far from here to Ngulipi outstation, where the cattle manager for the Balgo community lives. It has been Malley's job for some years now. During the Mongrel Downs years, when Malley was head stockman, he was part of the extended family of the station, and a role model for us children with his quiet good nature and wonderful horsemanship.

It will be good to see him and his wife Oriel again, but for the moment I need to sit and absorb the silence. There is real pleasure in choosing my own time and place to do this. In the past it was always someone else's decision. I made a promise to myself back then that one day I would come back on my own terms, and it seems I have kept it.

I led a double life during those years—a sixties schoolgirl wearing miniskirts and white lipstick, full of antiauthoritarian bravado, displaced in the holidays by a responsible young stockman, all frivolity banished, struggling to establish and maintain a place in the world of the station. I have talked to friends who also went from the country to boarding school, and they reinforce my experience. Teenage rebellion found its focus against the discipline of school life and the authority of boarding house staff. The normal struggle to separate oneself from parents was circumvented. Those brief bursts of holiday freedom were too precious to waste, and there was no precedent for conflict. The self-referential world of the station had shape and order. The value-shifting world of the urban sixties had no place here. I emerged from my boarding school years with the parental bond intact, while the other, independent self made its decisions and developed unhindered by reference to home and family. The independence took on an idealised, secretive form, not having been allowed to manifest its uncomfortably real shape within the family. In any case, to risk triggering in my father the soundless outrage of his disapproval was beyond me. It was easier to keep the worlds apart.

I was fiercely proud of my family and the life we lived, but at some deep level I knew even then that it was not for me. I didn't know what I wanted, but I knew I didn't want any of the women's lives I saw as I was growing up.

The white women I remember fell into two categories,

the active and the passive. The passive ones seemed on the whole more contented. I cannot tell in retrospect if they were happier. What I do remember is that men were responsible for most of the unhappiness of women. This seemed to be a given, accepted by everyone. Blame settled like an act of nature, before which everyone acquiesced.

Although there were always unattached white women in the country, the culture of the Outback was fundamentally masculine. This was still largely true in the sixties. To what extent it was actually misogynist I am not sure. There were, after all, so few white women to measure it by, and the Aboriginal women occupied a separate cultural and psychological strata which rendered the term almost meaningless. I had no real limitations placed on me for being a girl. The men I encountered, black and white, treated me with regard and affection. And yet I absorbed through my own skin and the antenna of adolescence a sense that to be female was to be subtly contaminated.

The young single women, home helps and governesses for the most part, moved in a haze of prurient conjecture and sexual innuendo (generated mainly by the men) which was only displaced when they struck up a permanent liaison with one of the men. The married women treated them with hostility and suspicion, which was frequently justified as there was a steady turnover of wives being displaced by nubile governesses. As a growing adolescent, to be a young female had a secret and forbidden potential. It offered the prospect of being bad without even trying. It was necessary for me to slide around and between the prohibitions, capitalising on a chameleon androgyny which concealed a lively and very female sexual curiosity.

It was not good to be plain, or opinionated, or overtly sexual, or incompetent. The women were, on the whole, as inclined to reinforce these prohibitions as the men, with the exclusion of the first.

There were women who were beyond reproach. These were usually older and married, strong decent women who took care of their husbands and children, never complained and could rise to an occasion when necessary, fighting bushfires, delivering their own babies, holding drunken intruders at bay. There were feisty women who did not take things lying down. The manager's wife at a neighbouring station had been one of these, and the row of bullet holes in the door of the station Toyota was frequently pointed out admiringly as evidence of her lively temper. Her husband had been in the vehicle at the time, driving off after a particularly fierce argument. Women like this usually developed into characters and made a niche for themselves as part of the local folklore, or became alcoholics and shrews, or walked out and never came back.

But most of the women I knew exhibited one or several of the undesirable characteristics and were judged accordingly. There was Esther, who was English, and did not wash. Esther was travelling, financing her passage by taking whatever work was available on stations along the way. This usually meant governessing, housework or cooking. Since she did not like children, was an indifferent cook and had a fairly cavalier attitude to dirt, she tended to move on fairly quickly.

Esther also liked men and was not backward in signalling her intentions towards them. My father, whose habit was to deliver an early morning cup of coffee to all the female members of the household, was confronted one morning with her large bare breasts greeting him exuberantly above the bedclothes. She had to forgo her morning coffee for the rest of her stay. Malley, who was head stockman at the time, came back from taking her riding looking pale and shaken.

She had fallen off her horse, and her shirt had somehow been torn off in the fall. What he could not understand was how her brassiere had also managed to come off. She was a big woman, and the sight of her half-naked six-foot frame was too much for Malley, who bolted, leaving her to get back on her horse and find her own way home. Esther was simply too big and too predatory. There wasn't a man on the place over five feet nine. Her sexuality was too visible for the sex-segregated culture of the bush, which preferred its activity to be covert or clandestine.

As for Albertine, she was homely and ridiculous from the start. She had patently come to the Outback to find a husband. I suffered for her because I liked her, but it was through her I understood the unassailable nature of misogyny towards the unattractive woman. Albertine was skinny, beaky and plain. She was also good-natured, kind and intelligent. She had a voice like a flock of galahs, and with all the affection of memory I cannot make her attractive. She found a husband no-one else would have. She was cheered for her success, and despised for it. She was pitied, because it was taken for granted that she would suffer and tolerate various forms of abuse. Knowing her husband, it is possible that people did him a disservice. I like to believe that Albertine's life was on the whole a happy one, within the limitations of what she expected from it.

How did it look to me, back then? How did I read the patterns and codes and hierarchies of the world as I experienced it? I remember a moment of vertigo, a jolt like a plane encountering turbulence. A young French woman was working on the station at the time. She was opinionated and forthright, not in the least flirtatious and entirely impervious to the local codes of behaviour. She stated her opinions without apology and frequently without tact. There was a particular occasion when she was holding forth about something, and the men were looking uncomfortable, when I thought—Doesn't she know to keep her mouth shut?, and in the same moment of feeling deeply embarrassed on her behalf I thought—What am I thinking? How has it happened that I am thinking this?

I might read the same moment differently now. It may have been that she was offering an opinion on something about which she knew very little. She may have been making a fool of herself and the men were too polite to contradict her. But my fifteen-year-old concern was for the breaking of rules which I had not understood existed until that moment. This was the taint I had smelled on my own skin, that we could not be relied upon, as women, to understand the rules properly, that our unruly bodies and emotions might force into the open things which would then have somehow to be dealt with.

MY MOTHER INSISTS THAT SHE was happy out here, most of the time. Her father came to visit once, a lovely Scotsman whose accent had hardly muted from forty or more years in Australia. Looking at her life, which seemed to be entirely taken up with managing the homestead and teaching children, he asked her if it was enough for her. Although he had been absent for most of her childhood, as a prospector and soldier and prisoner of war, he must have wondered at the transformation of the radical student and journalist who studied Arabic and Russian with the intention of becoming a spy, who defied her stepfather to go to university, who rode a motorcycle to her prenatal checks during her first pregnancy.

Here she listened to interminable discussions about stock and waters and mustering and fencing, and the edgy masculine gossip about the foolhardiness and bad practices of neighbours. She prepared or oversaw the preparation of three meals a day for family and staff, ordered the stores, did much of the bookwork and maintained a substantial vegetable garden. She taught her three youngest children, the children of the Aboriginal woman who helped in the house, and her elder son's friend who came for a holiday and stayed for two years. She came close to assaulting a census official who marked her on the census form as being an unemployed housewife. A born teacher, it was in the schoolroom that she could express all her enthusiasm and inventiveness. To my critical adolescent sensibility, which was trying to identify where it fitted in all of this, she was hostage to the homestead, patronised if she asked questions or attempted to move beyond what was considered her proper domain.

My mother answered her father's question as she always answered such questions, insisting that her life was full and satisfying. She was an inveterate maker of the best of her circumstances, not out of martyrdom and self-righteousness but out of a belief that since she was living it then it must be good.

13

A FEW MILD-FACED SHORTHORNS wander in for a late afternoon drink at Wilson's Cave, reminding me that if I am to reach Ngulipi before dark I should get on the road. If I am too late Malley will come looking for me.

When I arrive Malley emerges grease-stained and grinning from beneath the crate of a cattle truck, and greets me as if it has been weeks, rather than years, since we last met.

He has been in this country most of his life and knows it as well as anyone. His father managed Billiluna throughout his childhood and teens. His mother was a part-Aboriginal woman with a soft voice and a retiring, gentle temperament. The Aboriginal children who lived in the big camp near the homestead, people whose traditional country included the cattle station managed by his father, were his peers and playmates. He grew up speaking the language, and his father trained the Aboriginal boys to be stockmen with the same discipline and rigour with which he trained his own son. At eighteen, when my father gave him a job running the stock camp on Mongrel Downs, Malley brought with him the best of the black stockmen from the station which had been his home. They were like brothers and understood each other.

He was a shy young man, but in the bush and around the stock camp he had a confidence born of intimate knowledge of this world and its necessities. Now, in his late forties, he is a patriarch and a grandfather. His wife Oriel has hardly changed.

The Ngulipi homestead is built of sandstone, quarried locally. It is rather beautiful, low and rambling, with corridors and verandahs. Like many stone buildings it is full of private crannies and secrets. In the exposed red landscape it is a refuge for shadows. It was built by a robust and steadily expanding Catholic family who came to live and work on the mission during our years on Mongrel Downs. At first, advised by the incumbent priest that we were dangerous and not to be trusted, they were suspicious and reserved. A few meetings disposed of the suspicion, and the friendship survived the move of both families to Queensland.

The strained relations between Mongrel Downs and the mission had its origins in an incident which belongs to the early days of the stock route. I know the story by hearsay, but my father's diary account of the incident is worth recording as a masterpiece of understatement. It was the second big mob to travel the new stock route, and the diary suggests it was a desperate measure to shift thirsty stock from failing waters. The plan, I think, was to shift them only as far as Mongrel Downs, where they would provide the nucleus of the breeding herd.

Station diary. Friday, 25th October, 1963
Bill left with 1000 cows this morning.
Les carrying on shifting cattle between Old Station, Bungabiddy and Len's.

Wind drought. Cattle dying.
Arrived Bill's camp late night. Mess.

Saturday 26th
Bill's mob camped a mile away and perishing.
Discussed the cleanskin angle etc.
Have little hope of Bill's success in getting the mob through.
Saw them off camp.

Wednesday 30th
Went straight into Bill's camp and heard details about the smash with the cattle. About 100 perished.
Radio room. whip. radio. fainting blind gin. hospital. pics. sump oil. shower. chapel. big Sunday. tool box. engine room.
Will organise stock camp into getting another mob.
Called at Mission. Father wants his cattle next year now.

This is the story as I know it: the cattle were restive and thirsty, a thousand head of cranky cows who wanted to turn tail and go home. The drover in charge of the mob wasn't confident about getting them through. The cows weren't showing any signs of settling down, and the team of stockmen were local Aborigines the drover didn't know.

The mob began to string out, big strong cows in the lead sniffing the wind and walking out fast, and the tail of older and weaker animals falling further and further behind. Among the stockmen was one who had left his new young wife behind and was sorry now to be in the camp, wanted only to turn around and go back home. So he wasn't paying attention to the cattle, he was riding along behind the tail with his mind on his new wife and his grievances.

I may have this stockman confused with the one who was responsible for the cattle rushing into the big salt lake to the east, but if I remember rightly he had a wall eye and no wife. These stories always have a bad blackfellow or a mug jackaroo or a mad priest.

While this particular fellow was thinking about his troubles he wasn't noticing that some old cows had got onto a cattle pad leading into the mission and the rest of the tail was following behind. Before anyone realised what had happened, the old cows had got a smell of water and had broken into a trot. By the time they reached the mission precincts they were thirst-crazy and galloping. The first dozen or so sniffed out the water in a corrugated-iron communal shower. They crammed into it, licking at the taps and leaking shower roses, until the walls of the building burst apart and they threw up their wild old muzzles and galloped over the flattened sheets of iron and away down the road into the heart of the mission. By now there were a hundred or so cows on the rampage for any taste of moisture. Aborigines ran about shouting, trying to hunt the crazy cows out of their camps and buildings. A young woman abandoned the elderly blind lady in her charge, let go the stick by which she normally led her about, and bolted. A mass of snorting bellowing cows surrounded the old woman, lifting her along on a cloud of noise and dust and horns, so she must have thought that the fire and brimstone god of the Irish priest had got her at last. But the cows galloped on and left her behind, shrieking and cursing and unhurt, and the young woman crept shamefacedly back and took the spindly old arm and led her charge away.

The mission was built on a desolate flat, and the dust lifted and whipped between the buildings, so that when the dust arrived inhabited by red cows, it seemed as though they were some sort of corporeal manifestation of the earth itself. To the nuns, who found the country full of inexplicable things and privately considered it hell on earth, it came as no surprise that the dust should suddenly wear horns and tails. They shepherded together as many children as they could muster and took refuge in the chapel, after the bravest nun evicted a cow which had just guzzled the holy water from the font.

The holy father threw his hat and then an empty whisky bottle at the slobbering beast attempting to get through the door of his office, and used the kind of language only available to an Irishman and a man of God. It worked, for the cow turned tail and rushed down the steps and off to the mechanic's workshop, where she drank a drum of sump oil and fell down the pit and died.

The rest of the story is concealed in my father's truncated prose. I don't know what happened in the radio room; I don't know the fate of the toolbox or what big Sunday refers to. I do know that this episode cemented the bad relations between the priest, who we always referred to ironically as Father, and Mongrel Downs. For years afterwards it was war. Father was an adversary whose knowledge of the evil that dwells in the human heart provided him with all sorts of devious and underhand strategies to deal with those he saw as interlopers. Yet he and my father retained a reluctant regard for each other, and later my father always spoke of him with a sort of humorous affection.

Father was larger than life, with his own arrangements between the Lord and his whisky habit, and a real regard for the people under his care, whom he felt should be kept entirely protected from the outside world. The stories abound. He had been a boxer in his youth and took with him to the mission a set of boxing gloves and a pair of unpadded exercise gloves. The younger men set about testing the mettle of the new priest, this gingery Australian Irishman. He chose a smart and arrogant fellow and challenged him to a bout of boxing, offering him the advantage of the big gloves. It wasn't until the priest had landed several punches that the young Aborigine realised he had been tricked. The padded gloves rendered his own punches almost harmless, while his opponent's stinging blows were unimpeded. His peers were delighted at the cleverness of their new priest, and Father established himself as a man they could respect and admire.

Father moved on, or was moved, south, under a cloud the origins of which are too complicated to recount, and was replaced by Father Heaven (a more fortunate name than one Father Raper, who I believe spent time in New Guinea). Things settled down, and we no longer referred to the western border as the western front. But we missed Father. He was a wonderful villain, and life was not the same without him.

These days Balgo is no longer a mission, although the Catholic presence is still in evidence, mainly among the teachers. The cattle operation is run from Ngulipi outstation, about one hundred kilometres east of the main community, and the Aboriginal stockmen who work with Malley are the traditional owners of that part of the country. From Malley and Oriel's verandah I can see a campfire and a television set in the bare yard in front of one of the outstation houses, and a few dark figures sitting about watching the flickering screen. We talk of who is left in the country, who has died or moved on. Long Johnny Amaroo lives on Balgo now and has given Malley a message that I am to call in and see him. Johnny was one of the longest-serving of the Mongrel Downs stockmen, and in the earliest years my father's only companion.

WHEN I ASK AT BALGO FOR Johnny Amaroo I am told the name is *kumunjayi*. Someone called Johnny has died, and the name can't be spoken. It is Emaroo I am looking for. I am directed to the outskirts of the top camp.

Balgo community is located at the northern end of the immense Balwina Aboriginal Reserve, about nine hundred kilometres north-west of Alice Springs. It is set on a barren windy plateau which falls away suddenly into the eroded fortress of the Balgo Pound. The Pound is one of those natural features before which one can only offer silence. Superlatives are too fleshy, language too sensual to provide any meaningful interpretation of its sheer strangeness. It is a place which has been wrought by primordial excess. Everything about it seems fused, stripped, scoured. It is furred with spinifex, a yellowish-grey tinged with acid green. Its reds are burned and blackened, or leached and porous. It has been a sea, and has become a desert. The Pound itself is an extraordinary geological boundary, where one landform gives way precipitously to another. The flat sandstone plateau breaks away in a great arc, forming the edge of a remnant seabed whose fossil fragments are fused in blackened lumps of rock. Here and there on the ironstone plain the ancient plateau still clings to its sandstone cap, forming isolated clusters of mesas. Among the ironstone are hard black bubbles which have been forced by unimaginable heat, which the country still holds like a radiant echo. It is only on its immediate rim that you gain a sense of the depth of the eroded plain—once down on its floor the sheer immensity of the place reduces the scale of the surrounding plateau.

Johnny finds me before I find his camp. The word has gone ahead. His tall figure is instantly recognisable as he approaches. He embraces me, white-haired now, his face scarred from an accident in which a nun died. He launches immediately into the story, in which he was driving the mission Toyota. He tells me too that he got married, had a couple of sons, but his wife has left him. We sit by his camp, which is a roofless three-sided corrugated-iron structure, a few metres square, floored by a pile of blankets. Four or five mangy, scalded-looking puppies scuffle among the blankets. Johnny tells me he is painting now. I tell him that Malley has already shown me some of his work, and show him photographs of the rest of my family. We don't speak about my father. And then there is no more to say. This big, dignified man releases me. You can go now, he tells me, conscious of my whitefella awkwardness at ending the conversation. I would cry but don't want to embarrass him. Johnny was always getting into scrapes, getting arrested in town for drinking misdemeanours, having to be rescued. The police sergeant would release him into my father's or mother's custody without charging him, to get him out of town and out of harm's way until the next time. We children loved him for the time he took with us and the things he taught us.

—Which way that motorcar track going, Johnny?

—Might be . . . that way.

We would nod seriously.

—Or might be . . . that other way.

Deadpan, lips pointing along the track.

He was a different language group, different country from the other stockmen, and always a little apart because of it, too tall and gangling to make a really good horseman. I cannot imagine his life here in his corrugated-iron windbreak with his pile of blankets and mangy puppies. Does his painting sustain him? This is not his country, he comes from somewhere further to the south. His people have largely disappeared.

After the encounter with Johnny I retreat to the edge of

the Pound, out of range of the sliding sidelong glances of the people and away from the squalid fecund awfulness of the ubiquitous camp dogs. Sam has retreated in appalled disdain to his nest in the spare tyre, having glimpsed possibilities of a dog's life too horrible to contemplate. I need to be still, shut down the urgent conversation in my head, which insists—*It's too difficult, why are you doing this, let's get out of here.* A hard wind channels up the clefts of sandstone and beats against the metal sides of the Suzuki. The voice is scoured from my head by the abrasive air, leaving behind a raw and sensitive silence. From the plateau at my back, as the wind drops, come the sounds of young men playing football, the truncated yipe of a dog, a vehicle without a muffler hooning across the flat. Ordinary sounds. In a little while I will take the north road and head for the women's business. Meanwhile I try to fill in the neglected journal, using my father's trick of days and dates and blank spaces. But language has fled. I have effectively silenced the voice in my head, and there is nothing to say. The mapmaker takes up the thread, weaving her strange tale with the cross-threads of country and some loose end of my mind. The Pound's ancient seabed with its fossil memory of water is her territory.

The songs I know have spent too long in the mind. Like the maps, they hide the country from me. In these weeks of walking they have come apart, been shaken down into shapes of sound which echo the thud of a camel's hoof, the scraping of lizard's claws on rock, the high call of a hawk. Somewhere in the monotony of these repetitions is a language which reflects the country.

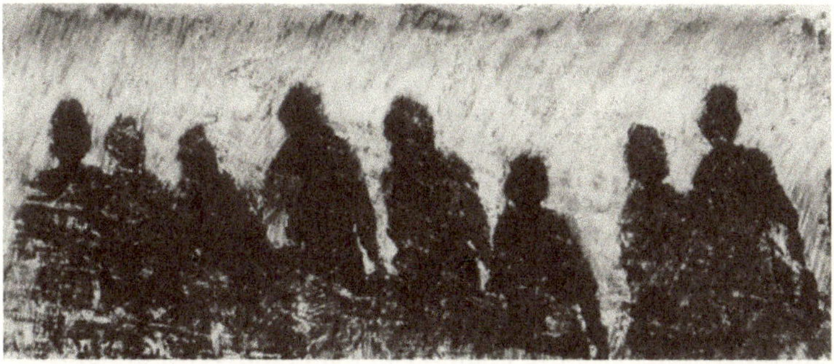

14

THE CHILD'S FIRST MEMORY was of black bodies, black skins, a warm, affectionate many-limbed creature of sagging breasts and sinewy limbs and tobacco-stained teeth. And with this memory came also the memory of being different, of her own tiny pale body amongst all the shining dark skin, of a difference which could not be annulled, which in spite of mud and ash and insect bites continued to emerge a pale translucent pinkish colour. Her parents were more or less the same colour, but flesh was not so manifest in them, it was always largely covered up and seemed to be a similar colour and texture to the clothes which contained it. It did not have the conspicuous *skinness* of these others, who tossed her about in the waterhole, passed her little froglike body between them, supported her kicking paddle among the waterlilies. Even the ones her own size were clothed by their skin in a way she was not, their grinning faces with gobbets of snot held precariously in place by upper lips. She could not achieve even this successfully, being constantly wiped clean on her mother's orders. So it seemed this most desirable state, to belong, could not be achieved, and she must learn to live with it.

Later she was to discover that a pale skin had many advantages, though it was an impractical colour for the climate, but by this time the habit of difference was ingrained. And the paleness proved infinitely permeable in the very young child, so that she absorbed through it the sensations and textures and odours of the place inhabited by her dark-skinned companions, and did not realise it was not the place inhabited by her own kind. As she grew older and spent most of her time among whites she forgot much of this, but a trace remained which made her reflexes always slightly out of kilter, as if her first responses sprang from a sensibility unfamiliar with the social language which surrounded her. Because of this she became acutely watchful and cautious, adept at anticipating and fulfilling people's expectations. Without deliberately contriving it, this provided a space within which she concealed her own fragile perceptions, which were able to survive intact.

She had two mothers, the white one who had borne her and the black one who named her and dreamed for her. The one who dreamed for her, her skin mother, gave to the child the dreaming of Pintapinta the Butterfly and named her for her own child which was never born. The child imagined the intensity of the light on the rust-coloured slabs of stone, the heat radiating out, butterflies clogging the hot air and covering the shallow edges of the tea-coloured water. She remembered nothing of the black woman's words, she had no idea what this totem conferred on her. All she had of it later was a sense of loss, especially piercing at the sight of butterflies, which blundered out of scented gardens in the heavy summer air and settled on her.

This time was almost perfect, except for the colour of her skin, which she tried to remedy with boot polish and paint, and was painfully scrubbed clean. Her white mother was romantic and delighted in her child's intense identification with this mysterious indigenous people. For a restless young woman unused to babies, they were a priceless source of childminding, and she readily relinquished the little girl into the black women's capable hands. Inevitably the child spoke first the language which surrounded her, and was fiercely frustrated that her white mother did not understand her. Later this white mother often reminded the child of this early gift of a dream, a name and a country, and the child accordingly cherished it as something which set her apart and made her special. She felt a responsibility towards her own singularity which she took seriously into adulthood, fending off the spectre of ordinariness with this talismanic knowledge.

THIS WHITE CHILD WITH HER skin name and her dreaming accompanies me along the sandy desolate track north towards Billiluna. I am Napurrula, which makes me legitimate heir to the country my father turned into a cattle station. I am aware of the spuriousness of all this. The conferring of a bush or skin name is given to everyone who spends time with the Aborigines, as a formality which places them in a category of relationships and behaviour. I would be deeply resentful of the same attempt to categorise me in white Australian society. So why do I cherish and honour this unearned title, which has been largely meaningless in the context of the life I have led?

I know why, of course. It gives me a link, a way of being here that circumvents my whiteness. It has allowed me to claim a kind of belonging that I have never felt. I have used it to claim a certain credibility among urban friends for my knowledge of Aboriginal society. It creates a frisson in the secular comfort of a suburban living room, provides a scrap of evidence that out there something authentic, chthonian, spiritual inhabits the continent. I have invested myself with its glamour. It is as if I have come by a secret password by dishonest means and have hoarded it against the moment when it might open a magic door. The door, when I arrive, has been open all along.

But it has provided something real too. Back then, when I received the name, when I was too young to remember, the country laid a claim on me which I cannot shake off.

Now that I am here I am embarrassed by it, reluctant to claim it. I know I am an imposter. I am confronted merely with a sense of difference which strikes me as being much more profound than I remembered. I have been away a long time.

THE CAMPSITE, WHEN I ARRIVE in the late afternoon, fills me with the familiar discomfort of all the times in my life when I have arrived alone among strangers. I am not supposed to be a stranger here, I have known this country since my childhood. The truth is, in spite of years of contact with Aborigines, I am always overcome by an extreme shyness in their presence. And I know them well enough to know there are all sorts of hidden etiquettes to be observed.

Making camp, I observe the Aboriginal tradition of camping in strange country in the direction closest to my own country. I do this automatically, as if a thread holds me which must be kept clear. I hunt for firewood, which is going to become a prime concern during the next few days. I am annoyed that I had not thought to throw some into the back of the Suzuki on the way to the camp. Wandering and looking, I am overtaken by the afternoon light slanting along the spiny edges of the spinifex and casting deep purple shadows. Such a clear light, and such dark shadows. I feel the anxiety leave me, as if it had never been.

<hr />

—Hello, dear. Where did you come from?

The speaker, a light-skinned woman in a pink dress, gives off an air of ingratiating gentility.

—Hello, dear. I'm camped in the green tent over there. Where are you?

—I'm on the other side, the yellow ute is mine.

I am noncommittal, feeling some kind of subtle demand in the woman's presence.

—Who are you with, dear?

She puts a hand out to take hold of my arm.

—No-one. I came alone.

—Are you by yourself, dear. You come and camp by me.

Her gaze floats around and past my face and she does not meet my eyes. Her smile bleeds away at the edges into lipstick-filled cracks. She is more white than black, this one, and wants me to know it. She is as out of her element as I am. But I know better than to be drawn into alliances of this nature.

—You come and camp by me.

But she has felt my withdrawal and given up already. She wrings her pale brown, rather pretty hands and backs away, her pink dress glowing in the sunset.

I say—Thanks, but I'm fine where I am. Thanks, I'm sorry.

—I'm sorry too, dear.

She continues to back away.

—You just come over to my camp if you get lonely, dear.

In the late afternoon light the campsite looks like a film set. Black figures in bright dresses and woollen beanies greet each other with shrieks and cackles, crouch over campfires, haul mountains of grubby bedding out of the dozens of white Toyota troop carriers. The cleared circle of deep red earth is lit by the falling sun in bands of brilliant light, the long shadows of women falling across it in slow elegant patterns.

As the darkness comes down a thin singing begins to seep out from the squatting groups, to collect and resonate at the centre of the circle. I remember the singing. It has always hurt me in some indefinable way, like the sound of curlews. A voice calls and is answered, calls again, and again is answered, until it becomes coated with layers of its own sound. It seems to contain and return its own amplified echo. The circle of fires and the chanting voices are suddenly piercingly familiar, and I fall through the gap of years into the desert night.

SOME TIME DURING THE EVENING I find Annette, the Balgo women's project officer who has organised the event. Annette is plump with pregnancy, harassed in a relaxed sort of way. Her major concern is the camp water supply. She leads me across to see the new portable corrugated-iron tank. The solder around its base has broken off in chunks, and water is running out unchecked. It is useless.

—I don't know what to do. The bore supply isn't enough. There's four hundred people here.

She looks fragile and exhausted. She is at least six months pregnant.

—There's a tank at the roadhouse, but there's something wrong with the tap.

—Maybe we can fix it. I'll come with you in the morning to look at it if you like.

The roadhouse proprietor also owns the station property on which the ceremonies are happening. He treats Annette and her project with amused tolerance. The tank, a robust steel structure mounted on its own trailer, needs a leather washer replaced at the tap connection. We drink tea in the large room behind the store. It serves as a kitchen cum dining room and the children's schoolroom. It is very familiar. The bare metal prefabricated walls and fly-wired windows, the scuffed lino floor, the touches of bright colour in curtains and tablecloth, children's drawings taped to the walls. The children watch and listen with bright curiosity for the moment which will include them. We establish common ground, talk about the ways in which the country has changed, who has stayed, who has moved on. These people are moving on soon.

—We've got the place on the market. Been made an offer by one of the local Aboriginal groups. Can't go against the way things are happening out here.

The proprieter is gauging me, to see how much I understand of things he will not spell out in Annette's presence. His wife speaks.

—We like it here. We love the country, you know. But it feels like it's time to go. And the kids will be in high school soon, it'll be good to be near a school.

They have scrupulously not said it. The country's gone to the blacks. We've hung on longer than a lot of others, but things are changing in ways we can no longer deal with.

On the drive back to the campsite Annette says—I've known them for two years and I've never had a conversation with them like that. It's like there's a wall between the station people and the whites who work with the blacks.

At the camp there is sorry business going on. For many of the women this is the first opportunity to get together since the deaths of family and friends, the first chance to carry out the ritualised grief which is part of the laying to rest of the dead. Groups of women advance towards each other, keening and wailing, clasp each other and bow heads and fall to their knees.

THE SINGING AND DANCING HAS been going on all day, with a repetitive monotony which cuts a groove into the brain. The dancing so far has combined something profoundly authentic with an impromptu awkwardness, like an unrehearsed chorus line. Bodies are exposed without self-consciousness, fat, skinny, glossy and nubile, ancient and leathery. Physical appearance seems to have little meaning. The ubiqitous woollen beanie exaggerates the line of a nose or brow ridge, but everyone is in skirts, except for a few of the white women. Most are wearing tights under the skirts for warmth. As the dancers heat up, blouses come off, brassieres are peeled down around the waist, and the slap of pendulous breasts syncopates with the thud of pounding feet. It is not serious yet, everyone is in a carnival mood, just playing. There are no dogs, apart from Sam, and only a few children, none of them boys older than four or five.

In the evening the tempo changes. The firelight simplifies and exaggerates the dancing figures, the bodies become iconic and marvellous. A young woman called Judith joins me in my camp. She is working on a project looking at major lake systems in Australia, and is here with a scientist studying Lake

Gregory. We talk about the strangeness of being white women in this place, the immense distance which separates our cultural experience from the one on whose perimeter we now crouch, the ambivalence with which we participate and draw back. We are neither of us comfortable. The gulf feels immensely difficult to negotiate.

THE CAMPSITE IS NEAR A BORE which Carranya Station's owner has given permission to use. Today they are helicopter mustering, and the pilot flew over the ceremonial ground, whether by accident or design no-one is saying. The site and the country within a radius of several kilometres is forbidden to men for the duration of the ceremonies. Within twenty minutes of the infringement the chopper came down. Fuel problems, according to the pilot, who was unhurt. The helicopter was a write-off.

THIS MORNING ONE SET OF dual wheels on the Balgo truck is flat. The tyres have been staked during a cross-country hunt for firewood. After a half-hearted attempt to undo the wheel nuts, the attempt to change the tyres has been abandoned. The responsibility to find a solution has been left to Annette. She enlists my help, and together we try to shift the wheel nuts, without success. I saturate them with CRC and suggest she finds a long piece of pipe for leverage on the next water run to Billiluna. Annette is looking increasingly harassed. The mill is no longer pumping because the kids have pulled aside the wire netting protection and dropped stones down the column. The bore will have to be pulled, a major operation which can't be carried out until the ceremonies are over. The lack of any toilet facilities is also making itself apparent, the campsite becoming ringed in ever-increasing diameters of human shit.

The women continue to dance, heavy bodies on thin legs, in shuffling, stiff-legged jumps, knees slightly bent. This step and the singing seem never to vary, as if the constant reiteration weaves and reweaves a pattern from which there can be no deviation. It can be woven with great skill, or poorly, but it does not change. The different dances are composed of different props, different arrangements, but the shuffling hop does not alter, nor does the curiously haunting lift and fall of voices which accompanies it. In the dance and in the song, time fragments. The rhythm of the circling feet becomes the stamping rhythm of ancestral women. Through the clear dense layers of the song their voices call the dancers in.

Some of the dances are light-hearted, mostly entertainment. Some are dark with hints of violence, some overtly sexual. During one of these performances, danced with broomsticks and a good deal of suggestive body language, the watching circle of women fling up a constant barrage of twigs, leaves and dust to clear away the spirits unleashed by the dance. Of the two principal dancers called in from the spinifex beyond the perimeter of the cleared ground, the younger woman is wearing black lycra cycling shorts. Most of the chorus line wear their woollen beanies, one has on sunglasses and sneakers, all are painted across the shoulders and breasts with white and red ochre. The performances are full of such incongruities, which at times border on the absurd. To me, the watcher, my perceptions are dislocated continually, the incongruities counterpointed suddenly by the dying fall of the voices, the puffs of dust which mark the boundary the dreaming spirits may not cross.

I wish I truly understood what is going on here. It is like reading a book whose real text is invisible. It was always like this, the sense of being on the outside of knowledge and language. One had one's own knowledge and language, which was difficult enough to manage, but something else was always taking place on the periphery of vision, within earshot but not quite comprehensible. I wonder if sheer discomfort is at the heart of prejudice.

Anna John makes me throw handfuls of dust in the direction of the dancers, to deflect the spirits and avoid being trapped in the dreaming. I ask her about the dances and ceremonies, but she says she doesn't know much, she is just learning about it now. Here in the midst of her traditional people, in her own country, she was raised on the mission as a good Catholic girl. Now I sit with her in the dust by her campfire, holding her newest grandchild, daughter of Julianne, who I held in the same way almost the last time I saw Anna twenty years ago. Julianne is now a plump young woman and this is her second child. Her little boy crawls over me, snotty-nosed and grinning, and Anna fishes a damper out of the ashes and offers me a piece. She tells me that she cried when she heard about my father's death. Rex, her husband, is still chairman of the local land council. Theirs is a story of true love. Anna, mission educated, could read and write, and would send letters to Rex when he worked on Mongrel Downs. Like most of the original team of stockmen, Rex came from Billiluna. He was an exceptional horseman, with a crumpled, worried face and a gentle nature. He was illiterate and would ask my father to read the letters to him and help him to draft his replies. Anna was wrong skin for Rex, and in order to marry her he went through a ritual spearing in the leg.

Anna has hardly changed, she is still tiny and skinny with a huge bush of hair. In fact she is physically very different from the other women, and I wonder whether she has some other blood somewhere in her background. Her manner is an odd mixture of gracefulness and brusque tactlessness.

I wonder why this journey has brought me into the presence of several hundred women who represent a basic, extreme form of femaleness. Their bodies are used, misshapen and damaged. So much flesh. Oiled and painted, it is magnificent. What am I supposed to make of these pared-down rituals in the desert?

Somewhere in my notebook is a quote from Charles Ponce. 'There is, in the psyche of mankind *and* womankind, an idea of something inferior, dark, weak, exiled and soulless.' An archetype of inferiority, projected onto the feminine. I touch this raw nub in myself and my hands come away bloodstained.

I IMAGINE MYSELF AS SOMEONE different, someone who meets life head on, who has fun. When invited by the women to be painted and join the dancing, she does it with respect and a light heart. She does not stand back self-consciously. This woman does not waste things. The taste of dust and ashy damper stay on her tongue with the taste of tea and the smell of burning gum leaves. She hears the creak of the windmill and the sound of women calling and splashing in the dam, and remembers the scent of childhood and the footprints of children in wet mud. This woman takes joy in life, and is not afraid.

Out in the spinifex the women sit in groups painting each other's bodies, heads leaning in towards one another, hands touching, rubbing, patting, marking. Above the grey-green mounds of the spinifex a circle of heads and arms move and sway like a single many-headed, many-armed creature. When I read their stories I feel as if there is a dimension missing. Maybe it is this dimension, of a shared knowledge so taken for granted that it has no words and therefore no place in the story. I read the stories and they don't touch me, but when I see them performed, that is something else altogether.

We have been given another piece of news about the helicopter pilot. I don't know if it is true, but the story is that last night his house in Perth burned down. His wife and child were unhurt.

THE NEARBY STATION OF Ruby Plains is supplying beef for the gathering. Each afternoon a girl drives in with a Toyota loaded with butchered beef. There have been mutterings about its distribution—apparently the bigger, more powerful groups are getting the lion's share and the small groups and old women are missing out. The spinifex windbreak is bristling with bits of bullock. Many of the white women are vegetarian and are giving the butchering area a wide berth. The growing pile of gumleaves onto which the meat is unloaded is beginning to look a little grim, if you are unused to seeing meat butchered on the hoof. It is the fourth day and there are now nine bullocks' heads gazing in mute bovine recrimination from the pile of leaves, and as many sets of shins and hooves, discarded at awkward angles as if trying to go somewhere away from all this.

This morning I attempted to organise it a little by hanging hindquarters and shoulders from wire hooks along the roof of the bough shed, so that chunks can be easily sliced off. Annette has asked me to oversee this afternoon's distribution, to see if it can be made a little more equitable. I enlist the help of two of the white women, Shannon and Emma. As the Ruby Plains Toyota pulls in there are already about a hundred women gathered and clamouring. We wade into the fray. It takes all the skills of placation and intimidation we can muster to give us some room to manoeuvre. I have given Shannon the axe. Her job is to chop through the bones, while I keep the butcher knife and identify good meat and rough cuts. Emma establishes who is who, how many in each camp, and I make lightning estimates of how much meat they need. Shannon chops with a will, long hair flying, and I slash rumps and topsides in a way that would make a butcher weep. He would weep even more to see what happens next—most of it will go straight into the beef buckets for boiling, though some is roasted directly on the coals. Emma is in the front line and taking most of the fire. The Pitjantjara mob from south of Alice are outraged at being subjected to such discipline. They are the largest and most powerful contingent, everyone holds them in some awe as they have a reputation for serious ceremonies and harsh penalties. But Emma stands her ground, and pretty soon all the meat has gone, save a few backbones with tails still attached. An old woman makes off with one of these clutched over her shoulder like a sack, skinny legs buckling under the weight. Shannon looks like a young red Indian warrior just back from a successful scalping expedition. I probably look pretty wild myself, butcher knife in hand and blood to the elbows. The three of us stand knee deep in gumleaves and carnage, adrenalin pumping, grinning at each other.

I have saved a fillet steak, thinking that the nonvegetarians may like some for the evening meal, but when I offer it at the *kardiya* camp (the Aboriginal term for whitefellow) they recoil from it and me as if I am some kind of monster. Suitably crushed I take it back to my own camp and eat in solitude. I hang the remains of the fillet from the canopy rack of the Suzuki, and some time during the night Sam steals it, adding to the growing list of his misdemeanours.

EMMA HAS TO MAKE A TRIP back to Halls Creek, so I go with her, curious to see what kind of town it has become. Emma's job has something to do with linguistics. Everyone I meet is associated in some way with the burgeoning industry of Aboriginal culture. They record stories and study language, assist in the production and sale of art, plan and build dwellings which take into account the needs and prohibitions of Aboriginal traditions. They undertake studies of the culture and the law. And so many of them are women. The male culture of the bush has undergone a strange sea change, and so have I. I have gone through the looking glass, and now I find myself pressed against the glass, looking back into the world I knew.

Emma bemoans the fact of cattle, mutters and curses as we pass through country showing the effects of drought and stock. It is too familiar to draw a response from me. She mutters and curses too at her own attachment to the country, says she needs to get away and get some perspective on her life. She is short and dark and attractive, full of bravado and vitality. I like her, with her sharp dry self-denigrating humour. Another refugee from the Melbourne climate (seasonal or psychological, I don't ask), she is beginning to show the wear and tear of this one. It is an old story, and one which the country spins out in endless variations, of a traveller who comes in search of a dream of glamour and splendid challenge and finds instead something intractable, uninhabitable and addictive.

I barely recognise Halls Creek, a small tidy place of lawns

and bougainvillea. I came here with my father the Christmas before I went away to boarding school. It was a strange, fraught visit, the culmination of a series of confrontations for which I only vaguely understood the reasons.

IN HER CHILD'S WORLD SHE is hardly aware of the adult business going on around her. A rumour of cattle theft seeps across the border. It is whispered that Joe Mahood has stolen four hundred head of cattle from Ruby Plains and has shifted them across waterless desert without leaving a track. Unchecked, such rumours become part of the country's folklore. The girl's father has no desire to become a legend of this kind and sets out to track the rumour across the southern Kimberleys to its source. It is nearly Christmas, time for the black stockmen to go back to their own country and start preparing for the big January ceremonies. The girl rides on the back of the vehicle among swags and stockmen, perched on the forty-four gallon fuel drum, absorbing a calligraphy of landscape as it unreels behind her. At one of the dinner camp stops Ferdie and her father broach the rum bottle and play a game of chess on the bonnet of the Toyota. Ferdie was a child chess champion back in Austria before his parents emigrated.

They stop at Carranya Station to talk to the owner, who has played his part in spreading the rumour. He implicates his neighbour, who is one of the local cattle kings. A big raw-boned woman tries to lift the drowsy child from where she has gone to sleep on the cool concrete of the laundry floor, but she fights away from this female concern, gone away into a world free of domestic boundaries. At Ruby Plains, from where the cattle had allegedly been stolen, the plot thickens and tempers fray. The station owner is not a man who takes kindly to being confronted. He places responsibility for the rumour with the stock inspector in Halls Creek. The girl's father insists that the owner accompany him to Halls Creek to speak to the stock inspector. The girl likes the man's wife, who is beautiful and lets her be.

The town of Halls Creek is red and muddy from recent rain, with a flotsam of rubbish along the edges of the main road. Malley's parents live in town, and his mother takes the little girl into the bathroom and shows her where she can wash and change. She is a gentle dark round woman, her voice softened with Aboriginal intonation. She would have made the child at home, but the girl insists on going with her father. He leaves her on the pub verandah in the charge of Pony Express and goes into the bar with Malley and Ferdie. Pony Express offers to shout her a beer, which she refuses, and then tells her his life story. He keeps losing the threads of it, until it is reduced to a tangle of loose ends in which even he loses interest. The girl has long since found a tattered magazine to read and curls up on a bench with the local dog for company and moral support.

She is hungry and bright-eyed when the men emerge from the bar, hilarious with some new song they have discovered on the jukebox. Ferdie sings the chorus in his Austrian accent.

When dem cotton balls get rotten
we didn t pick werry much cotton
in dem o-old cotton fields back home

He sings it over and over, and smiles his soft luminous smile. They carry her off between them like a princess.

The confrontation with the stock inspector solves the mystery of the stolen cattle. It seems he has mistakenly identified the earmarks of several Mongrel Downs cows as Ruby Plains on a trip across the border and has carelessly mentioned 'a mob' of Ruby Plains cattle on Mongrel Downs. The bush telegraph has done the rest. Her father is quietly satisfied that the matter has been cleared up and that people will be less inclined to bandy his name about in the future.

ALTHOUGH HALLS CREEK IS tidier and more substantial than my memory of it, it still has a makeshift feel. Emma's house is a fibro prefab balanced on steel stumps, the yard overgrown with dry clumps of yellow grass, the same grass that grows outside the cyclone wire fence and over the road and back into the surrounding scrub. The imposition of order on the straggling recalcitrant bush seems superficial and impermanent. So many Outback towns are a kind of mirage, given substance by a collective need for them to exist. The energy to maintain the idea of them ebbs and falters, and the towns at times become transparent, like film sets when the money has run out, and the actors are stranded in a drama that has mislaid its plot.

I should look for Harry as I know he is somewhere in town, but I can't face seeing him. This is a piece of profound cowardice on my part, which I know I am going to regret. I don't fully understand my reluctance, except to know there will be too much pain in the meeting for both of us. I have known Harry since I was ten years old. He, Rex and Malley were the mainstays of the Mongrel Downs stock camp, Harry taking over from Malley as head stockman when Malley moved on to manage Chilla Well. Across the gap of colour and culture we both know that lives go astray, fall apart, are patched together and reconstructed. People die out of their time and grief goes unnamed. We do not share a social language that will allow us to articulate this knowledge, but it looms between us with no room for any other thing to be spoken. I know he loved my father and my family. He knows we loved him. What can I say to him? I will do nothing but stand there and weep. I am on the brink of losing my nerve and my bearings out here. I must husband my tiny store of courage for what I still have to do. I deplore this abjectness in me and wish for more of the kind of courage that matters.

On the return journey to the camp we get a flat tyre, so it is sundown by the time we arrive. In the evening I join the white women at their campfire. Aboriginal women wander in, sit down for a while and talk, wander off again.

The talk is mostly about the business of working with Aboriginal women. It is refreshingly without constraint. There is no need to establish credentials. The mere fact of being here suggests a grasp of the ironies and contradictions which are an essential part of working in the fallout zone of cultural intersection. It is not necessary to edit the realities which must be spoken about so circumspectly in other contexts. The real work of these women is not written into the job descriptions of project or liaison positions.

—We're just white slaves, one of the women says cheerfully.

—We run our arses off and get burned out, and then come back for more. I don't know why we do it. For times like this, I suppose.

The perfect circle of the dark horizon, the bursts of singing and laughter from other campfires, answers the question.

Another woman speaks.

—The men don't like us. They think the women are getting too much power.

She tells the story of how on Balgo recently the men tried to get Annette dismissed. The women painted themselves up and marched through the community, forcing the men and boys to hide. The subject was dropped, but it continues to simmer.

I WOKE UP THIS MORNING with a weeping eye, so will try to see the nurse from Billiluna when she comes out today. The Yuendumu women are doing a major honey-ant dreaming dance, which has been going on for hours. Anne Mosey is with them, bare-breasted and painted up. Anne is an artist and has worked for a long time with the Yuendumu people. She has established a collaborative relationship with the Warlpiri artist Dolly Nampijinpa Daniels, and their work is shown in major contemporary exhibitions.

Shannon appears in my camp at regular intervals, drawn by the prospect of real coffee brewed in my espresso coffee pot. She is a beautiful ex-Melbourne waif who says she does not plan on making it past thirty. She has been sacked from Balgo and is now working with the women at Yagga Yagga in the desert south of Balgo, helping to record their stories.

—I don't know how to make the stories interesting to whitefellas, she says.

—Nothing happens. They walk along, somebody sees something, they sit down under a tree, they walk a bit further. The most exciting thing so far is when Tjama saw a sheep and thought it was a clump of spinifex walking around.

Shannon is good company, funny and mercurial and streetwise. She has about her a flavour of urban toughness that is familiar and refreshing.

The Western Australian Minister for Aboriginal Affairs is flying in this afternoon, so there will be a big performance tonight. At the moment the kids are rioting in the spotlight.

PATRICIA LEE COMES TO MY camp in the evening. She is Ronny Bumblebee's sister. The Tanami women are camped next to me, although I didn't know who they were when I chose this spot. Not such a coincidence, I suppose, as we come from the same country and chose the spot nearest to that place. Patricia and I have been watching each other ever since we became aware who the other was. Margaret is Patricia's mother, a very tall woman, stately and graceful. She is a big law woman. There is an old blind woman who crawls around, watched by the others. Usually she is led, or deflected before she comes to any harm. Sometimes, disgruntled, she crawls off and is left to her own devices, having worn out the patience of her caretakers. Somebody brings her back, having found her crawling among the feet of the dancers in the middle of the arena.

Patricia knows who I am.

—You grew up on Mongrel Downs?

—Yes.

She is a plump, strong, intelligent woman in her early thirties. Her daughter Beverly is here with her, a girl of about ten.

—Beverly was crying to come and see you today. I want to go and see Kim in her camp, she was saying.

—She can come, any time.

—Your father was killed in a helicopter.

—Yes.

She considers this.

She talks, tells me about the plans they have for Mongrel Downs, to establish a clinic, a little school. The soft, seductive threads of the story weave around me, draw me in.

—Maybe you can work for us. You can stay here. You know this country. Later we want to go to Inningarra, there's a woman's place down there. We want you to drive us.

We sit in the darkness, the campfire reduced to coals. Beverly has crept over and is sitting at her mother's feet. The words are part of the darkness, part of the country that folds around me.

—When do you want to go to Inningarra?

—In two months, maybe six months.

—How many want to go?

—Maybe twelve. Some old women from Lajamanu. Maybe fifteen.

—It would need more than one vehicle.

—We can get the Balgo Toyota.

The Balgo Toyota is a point of contention. Whenever the Tanami women borrow it, they refuse to give it back. There is nothing in the world as desirable as a Toyota. Toyota dreaming is beginning to crisscross the country. I want to do the Inningarra trip, but I know it would be hell to get two overloaded vehicles of mostly old women through the trackless spinifex down to the Inningarra range and back. Not that I am afraid of getting lost. Some of the women know the route, and their recall of country is peerless.

Patricia tells me there is a path of important sites through the eastern part of Mongrel Downs, through Lake Ruth down to Inningarra. I tell her I have commitments in Queensland but that it might be possible for me to come back. Part of me wants to stay, wants to submit to this deep subtle grip of the country and its people. It feels like fate is coming full circle. But at the same time I cannot trust this desire, contaminated as it is with all kinds of baggage and sentiment. There is a saying in the country that the whites who work with the Aborigines come in three categories. Missionaries, mercenaries and misfits. I wonder where I would fit? Possibly a touch of all three.

I do not want to come back here. I do not want to live here. I came back in order to free myself from this place, but it leaks through my bloodstream like a disease.

IT IS STILL DARK WHEN Patricia wakes me and takes me to sit with the Tanami women. This is the big performance. This is when the dreamtime is invoked and made visible even to outsiders like me. I crouch down with the women. It is bitterly cold, and small fires spring up everywhere. After the casualness of the past few days there is an intensity of focus which is palpable. I am tucked in, close and warm, bodies leaning into one another. Beverly has crept in under my arm, Patricia sits next to me and tells me the story as it unfolds.

The singing begins, a sound that wells like blood or water from the ground. They are singing the country, and the country sings back. That unearthly, familiar sound collects in several hundred throats, resonates and fades, building to an intensity which must invoke some sort of manifestation, and does. Outside the cleared circle in the rising dawn two naked figures advance. They wear hair-string veils and loincloths, their bodies glisten with oil and ochre. One of the dancers is Margaret. I recognise her because of her height. But it is Margaret transformed from the graceful, gentle, homely woman in a cardigan and woollen beanie to a figure of hair-raising power. The bodies loom out of the dreaming with a form that matches the forms of the country. I want to weep for the beauty of these women, and my teeth are chattering violently. Behind the singing the watching women begin to wail and sob. Patricia tells me they are weeping for these ancestral women who travelled through this place and are dead now. An archetype of femaleness is stepping its truncated rhythms in the half-dark, raising puffs of powdery dust. The seated watchers fling up handfuls of dust and the wailing intensifies as the dancers approach. I want to howl, crawl, tear my clothes. I hug Beverly, and feel icy tears on my face. I am seeing the ancestors dance, but they are not my ancestors.

The women fade back into the dawn. The dance is over.

And now it is our turn. Everyone has red ochre rubbed onto the face and arms. Sarah, who is a law woman and healer for the Tanami mob, takes my face and hands in her little claws and rubs the ochre into my hair and skin. Patricia is plastering all the vehicles with it. Once the binding agent for the ochre was goanna fat, but now it is cooking oil in plastic containers, which litter the campsite from end to end.

Shannon comes looking for me. With her hair and arms dyed red she looks more than ever like a red Indian. I feel as if I have been branded. I brew a coffee, ask her for a cigarette. We sit by the fire and watch as the camp begins to break up and mobilise. The ceremonial objects are assembled and carefully packed away. Most of them seem to be kept in broken vinyl airline bags.

Patricia tells me they have been deciding on a skin name for me. I tell her I am named already.

She asks me—Who was your skin mother?
—Nancy Napaldjari.
—You Napurrula then.
—Yes.
—I told you, she tells the others.
—I told you she was Napurrula.

Patricia and Beverly are coming with me in the Suzuki. In fact the whole mob seem inclined to crawl aboard, but there is simply not room. One old woman is folded up and poked in on top of the load beside Sam, the rest are to come in the Balgo truck. The cavalcade sets out for Billiluna, about forty vehicles in all, mostly Toyota Landcruiser troop carriers. All the vehicles are daubed with red ochre. We look like a tribal migration in a Mad Max movie. The Balgo vehicle won't start, and some of the women are left behind. Patricia takes the small truck back to pick them up, but there is a fiasco of boiling radiators and broken down vehicles, and the final ceremony at Billiluna takes place with both Patricia and Margaret absent. A small group of men sit cross-legged on the ground, looking distinctly uncomfortable, while four hundred women dance slowly past them, singing and brushing them with branches.

This noisy, lackadaisical, unromantic horde of women flies in the face of the mythic convention of the laconic white male protagonist who moves alone through the landscape, reading its mystery and responding to its imperatives with stoicism and competence. I recognise my father in this convention. Most of these women would not dream of moving alone through the country, Aboriginal people being susceptible to and easily frightened by its manifestations. But the black women effortlessly marshal its energies to protect their mysteries, and the laconic hero, in the guise of the helicopter pilot, is vanquished almost as a side effect.

LATER I ASK PATRICIA IF it is all right to write about the ceremony. A book for *kardiya*, I tell her, so whitefellas know that the black women are still strong. She considers this.

—You can write what you saw. You can write about the dancing and the singing and how we come together to share the dances and for family and telling stories. You can tell the *kardiya* how we come together for the country.

Margaret says—You are lady and you belong to the country. You can write down story for the country.

15

My father briefly managed Billiluna, acting as a sort of travelling overseer while bores were being sunk and the homestead site established on Mongrel Downs. It was during this time that my father and Bill Wilson, the owner of Billiluna and partner in Mongrel Downs, returned to the homestead to discover the staff had been on a drinking spree and had broken into the house.

The Billiluna break-in belongs to the early pages of the station diary. I have heard the more dramatic tales of those days many times. I had always imagined them occurring over a period of months or years, each event self-contained, strung at sensible dramatic intervals along the storyline. Instead, when I examine the details in the diary I discover them telescoped, overlapping. The mad cow assault on the mission occurs at the same time as the break-in, the plane crash on Lake Ruth a few days later. It was a busy week.

Billiluna was in one of its feckless frontier phases, with a motley selection of itinerants working as ringers, horsebreakers, boremen and the like. The boundary between order and anarchy, always fragile in these outposts, needed only a nudge from alcohol to breach it. Everyone was somewhat sorry for themselves in the aftermath of the break-in, and there was little resistance when Bill and my father loaded them onto the truck and took them into Halls Creek police station, although several had to be handcuffed to the tray. As always my father does not elaborate, beyond the mention of the piece of trace chain wielded by Bill Wilson and the 22 pistol, or squirt, which my father generally carried in the door of the Toyota.

> Station diary. Saturday, 26th October, 1963
> Bill's mob camped a mile away and perishing.
> Discussed the cleanskin angle etc.
> Have little hope of Bill's success in getting the mob through.
> Saw them off camp.
>
> Back to station and found house broken into.
> Sacked mob.
>
> Sunday 27th
> On radio.
> Sacked Elsie and took the staff to Hall's Creek police station.
> Bill Wilson had some trace chain and I had a squirt.
> Charged them with breaking and entering.
> Stayed out of town.
>
> Monday 28th
> Got stores. Straightened out the cheque business.
> Blokes all got 20 pound fines and costs. Two of them got supply charges and are in for 3 to 6 months.
> We're not very popular at the moment.

One of the miscreants, who received a sentence of several months for breaking and entering and for supplying alcohol to Aborigines, howled at my father through the bars of the Halls Creek lockup.

—Hooshta, you Afghan bastard. I'll follow you to Alice Springs if I have to to lay strychnine on your tucker!

It was a common assumption that Mahood was an Afghan name, and my father had the colouring and profile to make it convincing. A few months later the same man asked for a job on Mongrel Downs. He twitched and shuffled his feet, the light of a poisoner in his shifty eyes. He didn't get the job.

The old Billiluna homestead is gone, burned down some time in recent years. It is where I spent my first Christmas in this country, en route to Halls Creek on my father's quest to silence the cattle-thieving rumour. The homestead was made of concrete and tin, full of dark interior rooms, most of the life lived on the concrete slab verandah which extended on all four sides of the house. The verandah was cluttered with perfunctory bits of furniture—various battered armchairs and benches, a number of cyclone stretchers without mattresses, on which guests could throw their swags. The kitchen was located some distance from the main homestead, in case of fire, an ineffectual precaution as it turned out.

CHRISTMAS DAY IS AT BILLILUNA, with the Adamsons. There are numerous Adamson kids and black and white staff members, as well as the Mongrel Downs contingent of Aboriginal stockmen, Malley, Ferdie, the girl and her father. This is where most of the stockmen come from, so they have gone down to the camp to take on their traditional roles and responsibilities. For the next couple of months their lives will be spent in the bush on ceremonial business.

There is a present for the little girl under the tree.

Someone has remembered, and her package contains the same articles as the presents for the Aboriginal housegirls—scented soap, a face washer, a coloured bandanna. She is delighted, particularly with the bandanna. In the afternoon some of the men bullfight on the lawn. They get down on all fours and snort and bellow and throw up clouds of dust, then lock imaginary horns until one of the protagonists is driven backwards by the weight or strength of the other. Ferdie and the girl's father invent a new dance called the Mongrel Stomp. The dancers face in opposite directions and lock necks and shoulders together, high-stepping in a circle until the feet of each dancer get further and further apart and the whole structure collapses on the lawn. Ferdie giggles and collapses immediately, but Malley is agile and can maintain his balance for a long time.

MALLEY HAS TOLD ME THAT Harry and Daisy's son Anthony is living at Billiluna, married to a girl who is almost white, and has two small children. There is a queue at the store, and while Shannon and I wait I notice a young man driving a white ute. There is a look about him that reminds me of Daisy—straight fairish hair—a fineness of feature that is Harry's. It has to be Anthony, and when I see the little fair-skinned girl with him, I am sure. I watch for a while, curious as to what I will find to say to this young man whose early life was so bound up with my family, who as a child sat at the table and called my father Dad because everyone else did.

When he comes into the store I ask him—Are you Anthony Hall? He is startled, says yes. I tell him who I am and ask him if he remembers the family, remembers coming to Queensland with us. He says yes, he remembers. He is surprisingly small, both his parents were quite tall people. He tells me he is learning to be a teacher and that his father is living in Halls Creek. There is really not much to say, this young man has nothing to do with the delightful child we all loved. I don't ask him about his mother, because I don't know if she is dead or alive. I ask him to tell Harry when he sees him that I was asking about him.

There is a general exodus now, vehicles begin to pick up their human cargo and head out, north-west, south-east. The two staked tyres on the Balgo truck have to be mended, so I stick around to lend a bit of moral support to Annette and Shannon.

Shannon attacks the tyres with the bead-breaker, gets them off the rims, and pregnant Annette pulls out the tubes, finds the holes, attaches vulcanising patches. The Balgo women sit in a nearby patch of shade playing cards. Shannon is in bad odour with them for throwing all the swags off the back of the truck. I get annoyed that they don't lift a hand to help, and more so when there are no tools in the truck and mine are borrowed. Annette says she can't leave tools in the vehicle because they immediately disappear.

A couple of the women have come to help with the tyre-mending, and now I am watching out for my tools. This makes me feel like a neurotic whitefella, but I can't risk the trip with any tools missing. I know I don't have the temperament to work out here with these women. It would turn me into a martinet and a fascist.

The tyres are mended, a second wheel is put on the rear dual set and the truck is reloaded. But no-one is ready to move. There are card games to be finished, exchanges to be completed. It is not time yet. The energy to move accumulates slowly. Somebody collects something and throws it on the truck; someone calls out to a small group sitting in the shade some distance away. Several younger women wander back towards the store. Grubby bundles materialise. Cards, money and tobacco are stuffed into a remarkable assortment of handbags. With no discernible transition things are happening. The truck is loaded, boarded, moving. It happens when it is ready to happen.

AT BALGO I TRACK DOWN Sandy, a young schoolteacher at whose house I am to spend the night. I park the Suzuki close to the mesh-enclosed verandah and unload most of its contents onto the verandah. There is a band of kids who spend most nights on the rampage around the community, and stealing from visitors' vehicles, or stealing the vehicles themselves, is a favourite diversion. I am carrying two jerrycans of petrol, which is no longer available on Balgo since petrol sniffing reached epidemic proportions.

Sandy grew up in the north, was educated in Perth and has come back to the country to teach. She loves it but acknowledges the almost insoluble difficulties it faces. We talk of our own ambivalence, our backgrounds in the pastoral industry, our urban education, the influences which pull in so many directions and contradict one another. How it is impossible to come back and belong to it fully and unquestioningly, how it is impossible to go away and leave it behind. We talk too of the traps of mythologising, how endemic it is in this environment. She tells me a story of a young man she knows. He had a strange and remarkable adventure, which he survived with endurance and courage. The story was retold, written and filmed. These days he lives in the character created by the myth and is a parody of the resourceful boy whom the adventure befell.

Shannon arrives late, to shower and change. She is persona

non grata at Balgo and will take the Balgo truck with some of the women down into the desert outstation at Yagga Yagga tomorrow morning. I roll my swag out and sleep on the verandah near my gear.

Over breakfast Shannon tells me hair-raising stories of her life in Melbourne. I try to convince her that life after thirty has its compensations. I am sad to say goodbye to her, but we are bound to meet again some time. Long Johnny is at the store, and we say our goodbyes. He chooses a photograph of my youngest brother Jim and his baby son as a memento.

BALGO IS A DIFFICULT PLACE, one of those locations where one feels something volatile and even inimical in the landscape itself. The community is a confrontation between all that is still alive in traditional culture and all that has gone wrong with the various religious and political forays by whites into the troubled terrain of white–black relations. Whitefellow dwellings all have steel mesh enclosing the verandahs, and the whites live in a state of quasi-siege brought about by petrol-sniffing youths. Fuel bowsers look like trapped Daleks, immobilised in multiple layers of welded steel. It is Garcia Marquez country, surreal, larger than life, alarming. The fact that it continues to produce vivid and remarkable art is a homage to the people who, in spite of extraordinary difficulties, maintain a profound and vital link with their country and their heritage.

Before I leave I look at the selection of paintings in stock. Many of the best artists, who know the law and the country, will not go back to the country it is their right to paint. They are old, dependent on others to drive them, and the lives of the younger people are taken up with other things. The stories of country are here now, on canvas. Some of the journeys they depict have not been travelled for a long time. But the knowledge will remain, transcribed in paint. The paintings have become the journeys they no longer make to their ancestral sites. The dots and lines and circles that describe waterholes and bush tomatoes and yams and dreaming tracks are more and more a form of imagined or remembered journeying.

Some of Johnny's work is here, but it is not what I am looking for. I choose a work in which a rectangular inner boundary encloses the main features of the painting—human and animal tracks, and claypans of a vivid acrylic blue. The boundaries which have been making themselves felt in my own work are felt by others. There is a reproduction of a work by one of the best-known of the Balgo artists. She uses a squared-off motif to designate claypans. The painting is a grid of linked squarish forms, asymmetric but perfectly balanced, with dark centres and ribbed edges of ochre and green. It is the abstract space which I continually encounter, impenetrable and irresistible.

It is odd to think of the fate of many of these paintings. They go, the best of them, to galleries and collections all over the world. A nondescript piece of ironstone country, punctuated with a claypan and the guttering trench of a small gully, will quietly dominate a New York living room. Many of the people paint, though some are better than others. They paint for money, but in spite of the income they receive the economy of their lives does not seem to change very much. One feels beneath the surface of the culture in this place the intractable oppositions of thought structures, of ways of understanding the world, which have ground helplessly and inevitably into each other.

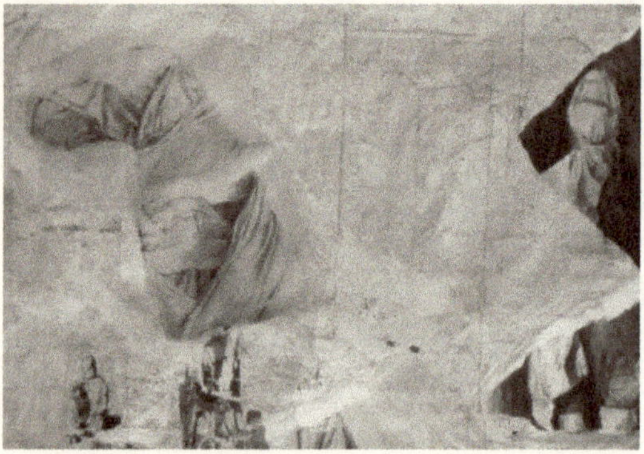

16

THE ROAD BETWEEN BALGO and Ngulipi is a channel of pink sand. Long blue escarpments dominate the horizon. As I approach the double landmark of Ngali Kudgera, the Two Hills, known in my father's time as McGuire's Gap, it shrinks to low hills with a vivid stand of ghost gums at the base. Davidson remarks disgustedly in his journal on this habit of the country to mislead.

> Sighted the supposed high mountain ranges, some twenty miles out of position. These proved a wretched failure, being nothing but a short run of low hills . . .
> The Basalt Range was like the high mountain ranges—a fraud—proving to be a sandstone and grit tableland . . . Gave the geological map of the Territory best after this failure.

These sentiments are echoed in my father's stock-route report as the land party inches its way west through sand bog and drizzling rain.

The sandstone hill was the best landmark for thirty miles around, but it wasn't marked on our aeronautical map. As it was only thirty miles off the Tanami road it didn't give us much confidence in our maps for the rest of the trip, as the only landmark shown anywhere near our route was noted 'position doubtful'.

The country continues to slip through the nets with which we attempt to control it. One morning when my family was still living out here my mother intercepted a distress call from an expedition lost somewhere near the border. She helped them locate their position and asked them who they were. The somewhat embarrassed reply identified them as a field team for National Mapping.

The ghost gums at the feet of Ngali Kudgera are too good to pass by, so I pull off the road and boil the billy in their broken shade. I spread out all my maps and they are cool and green, a symmetry of grids which keep the country in order. If I can find my place on the map I am safe from all this dry red space which surrounds me. So long as I can stay inside the map, I can imagine myself reaching any point on it. I am here on this thin dotted line a few centimetres from the edge of the map, which ends at the 129th parallel. That edge tells me I am a stone's throw from the Western Australian border, somewhere around the heart of the dead sheep with its legs in the air that is the shape of Australia. I sit in the red dirt at the heart of the dead sheep with all my maps spread out around me.

My maps are all green rectangles, but the space I see from where I am sitting is a red circle. I begin to draw on the clean green paper, pushing graphite and ochre and dirt into the glossy surfaces until the grid lines and names and locations are lost under a layer of earth and spit and pigment. Now the maps look like the place I can see.

But the other maps, which chart invisible country, are not so easily remade. Like mediaeval Mappaemundi, with their mythical beasts and fabulous journeys and their aspirations to provide a moral order, they shift with the terrain.

> *The first part of the journey was undertaken with little idea of the hardships to be endured. The journals and maps of our predecessors prove to be misleading, describing landmarks at once familiar and strange, as if they came upon them from a different aspect. At times it seems we are travelling through an altogether different landscape from the one described by the maps we carry.*
>
> *We travel from daylight to dark and seem to make no progress. The horizon torments us with images of water. In this country of shifting landmarks the light plays strange tricks, investing the landscape with mirage and apparition. It seems we have been travelling forever. It is at times difficult to remember why we embarked on this journey.*

The gaps of silence through which the mapmaker's voice makes itself heard have been filled these last days with the sounds of women singing. Her voice speaks from the place where maps reflect like water and conceal strange depths. Between the twin hills a band of travellers passes. Once I might have pursued them, calling out for them to wait, to tell me their purpose and their names. Now I sit quietly in the shade of ghost gums and leave them to their own journey. I know well enough that our paths will cross again.

I ARRIVE AT NGULIPI HOMESTEAD early in the afternoon and wash most of the red ochre off the Suzuki, leaving some as a protection for the rest of the trip. We spend the evening talking, until it is time for Oriel to go and watch one of the television soaps to which she is addicted. It is possible to get three channels out here now. Here among people who knew me twenty years ago an identity is gently forced onto me. It sits awkwardly, like an ill-fitting dress. I ring a friend in Sydney and we talk for a long time. Briefly I have the illusion of familiarity, that there is a real world somewhere to which I belong. But when I put the phone down it feels like just another badly fitting garment, of a more contemporary cut but still made for someone else.

In the morning I walk down to the yards, where for the last couple of years Malley has organised a local rodeo. From the number of dried-out carcasses littering the flat, the attrition rate on the animal participants is pretty high. On the other hand they may have died in the drought. There is a curious-looking structure nearby, rather like a Hills Hoist mounted on a hexagonal steel frame. It proves to be a primitive merry-go-round, with a rotating bar which can be attached to a motor. To ride on it a child would have to perch on the metal crossbars and cling to the central pole. This pared-down artefact from the iconography of childhood pleases me. Beside it lie two cow skulls. I cannot resist suspending them from the frame. It gives the merry-go-round a satisfyingly ironic and faintly sinister quality. Away on all sides stretches the red ironstone flat, punctuated by a scatter of white bones and shrivelled rust-coloured hide.

Do all children recognise in merry-go-rounds this quality that is both magical and sinister. The first merry-go-round I remember was a wagon wheel on its side, pinned into the red sand 'playground' of the Finke school. Finke, on the edge of the Simpson Desert, was little more than an idea continually being rescued from the hurtling flurries of red dust which threatened to cover it. It consisted mostly of sheets of rusty corrugated iron held down by old tyres.

The playground was limitless, but by a kind of local consensus it went to the edge of the long low sand ridge which stretched away behind the school. We would ride the wheel, feet kicking to keep it spinning, hanging on until prised off by others waiting for a turn. Sometimes my mother, who had established the school, chased a recalcitrant child over the dune when he decided he had had enough of school. She could run like the wind and always caught him. She would have been just over thirty.

When I dig for the origins of my view of the world, or of an aesthetic or mythical sense of the land, I always find myself back at Finke. When my family went there I was two and a half years old. It is the first place I remember clearly. Right through the fifties the Centre was in severe drought. Finke, situated on the north-western edge of the Simpson Desert, where the Finke River begins to channel its way out into the true desert, was always in danger of disappearing under the weight of drifting red sand which blew in off the desert. A single strand of wire was enough to cause a dune to build up over time, and fences always had a heaping of sand along them which slowly crept higher and higher. After a really good dust storm the drinking water in the tanks was stained red and a film of dust had infiltrated between the bed sheets. The red dust of the desert was a perpetual element in our lives. We drank it, we slept in it, we breathed it.

My parents and I lived at first in one of the fettler's cottages, the characteristic fibro railway houses that one saw with their backs to the railway in every community along the line from Adelaide to Alice Springs. My father's jurisdiction as stock inspector covered a large part of the Territory south of Alice. Our neighbours in the other cottages were fettler families. They were a cosmopolitan lot, part of the 1950s assisted migrant scheme which required a two-year national service on the immigrants' arrival in Australia. There was a German family, and a Czechoslovakian family, and a couple from Southern Italy who spoke almost no English. There was usually also one of those itinerant poor white families who drifted along the line, never staying too long anywhere, the six or seven or eight children gleaning bits and pieces of education where it was available. It was the arrival of such a family in Finke a year or so after I reached school age that provoked my mother to establish the school, for she could not stand to see children not being educated.

The father of the German family told us how they came to arrive in Finke. Back in Germany he had been given a choice of locations along the Ghan line and along the line which ran across the Nullabor. On his map of Australia he could see that the town of Finke was located between two big rivers, the Finke and the Goyder. He thought that since he was uprooting his family and taking them off to the new world, he could at least take them to a place where there was water and greenery and nice places for picnics on weekends. The rivers did not run at all in the two years the family spent in Finke, and he would look out across the treeless wasteland to the south-west and the spinifex-covered dune to the east and shake his head and chuckle.

The Czech father was not so philosophical, and he lacked humour, so he drank a lot and beat his wife and daughter from time to time to cheer himself up. What I remember of those railway houses is how much the same they all were, and yet how subtly different. The German house was light and bright, while the Czech house was dark and grim and depressing. I would not go inside, in spite of the fact that the daughter was my friend. The Italian house was friendly, an easy place for a child to visit, and I do not remember the lack of language being any sort of barrier. However, when I discovered the kid goat pegged in the back yard was to be killed and eaten, I enlisted my tiny brother's help to steal it and take it back to the goat yards. The poor white house was a wreck, flywire pushed out, piles of cans and rubbish thrown off the edge of the verandah, the yard a dustbowl scattered with broken toys and discarded clothing.

A government decision determined that the stock inspector's new residence be built on the site where the local mailman had his camp. The town's Aborigines camped there as well, so the area was a cluster of humpies, old sheets of tin, scattered bits of the mailman's defunct trucks and the general detritus of an Aboriginal camp. Rather than alter the site for the building, bureaucracy decreed that the mailman and the Aborigines had to move, which they did, as far as the boundary of the new dwelling.

This frontier is the measure of my childhood. I am standing on the pristine flywired verandah of our new house, looking across the red sandy expanse of the back yard. A cyclone-wire fence delineates the boundary between the domestic order of my home and the dangerous vitality of the camp. To begin with the anarchy is held at bay by the fence, although the frequent dust storms plaster sheets of rusty corrugated iron and scraps of ragged clothing along its length. And then the wind begins to worry at the sandy hummocks that have been fenced in, and strange buried things come to light. The back yard is a treasure trove of ancient truck parts. An entire chassis emerges like the bones of a squat and clumsy herbivore, some tortoiselike giant beast trapped by sand as it grazed slowly across the spinifex. The remnants of an ancient mechanical civilisation are exposed—truck springs, old batteries, carburettors, radiators. And then another storm blows in and buries it all again.

Meanwhile the life beyond the fence goes on. The camp dogs tear to pieces a joey kangaroo pulled from the pouch of a doe brought back by the hunters. Naked children pilfer chunks of damper and charred goanna from the coals of the cooking fires. The blue smoke of campfires punctuates the red clouds of approaching dust storms. From my verandah the skies of my childhood are filled with portents.

There is a steady traffic between the camp and the house. The mailman's de facto Aboriginal wife comes to help my mother in the house and look after my little brother. She also has a proper Aboriginal husband who is the mailman's offsider and the father of her third son. Her eldest son is the result of her rape as a girl by a white pastoralist. My mother collars this child, literally reaches over the back fence and pulls him across to join me in the makeshift classroom on the verandah, where she has begun to teach me by correspondence. This is before the arrival of the publican with his wife and five children, the fettler's straggling tribe, the Germans and the Czechs. We are the only school-age children in the town. With the arrival of my brother I have lost my status as the town's only white child.

In the mornings the little Aboriginal boy sits at the school desk my father has mended and painted and learns to read and write. I take a certain satisfaction in my superior skill in this area. In the afternoons I climb the fence into his world, and the roles reverse. Here I am always the one who doesn't know. We go for long walks in the sandhills, and he shows me a plant with a taproot which can be chewed for water. His mother teaches us the stories scribbled on the dunes.

Every track tells the tale of a particular creature. The desert, which in daylight seems populated only by crows and camels and lizards, is a place full of nocturnal adventures.

We visit the groups of card-players who sit in the only substantial shade available, cast by the huge steel railway tank which provides water for the Ghan. I share my first chew of pituri, a mildly narcotic weed which is mixed with coolibah ash and kept in wads tucked behind the ear. The Ghan arrives at intervals, a mysterious visitant from another world, and the passengers stare curiously from the open windows of the carriages. When the train has gone we put our ears to the steel tracks and listen to the sound which travels along the line long after the train has disappeared.

AT MALLEY'S REQUEST I PAINT a logo of an Aborigine spearing a bullock on the door of the Ngulipi cattle truck. Later we drive down to Buffalo Hole, at the beginning of the salt-lake country. Approaching it we come to a watercourse winding through dense ti-tree, and I recognise a place described by my father. He walked through it with several of the Aboriginal stockmen one afternoon, searching for the waterhole. Some domestic pigs had been released in the area and gone wild, and the stockmen were very nervous. At one point when they were separated from my father on a parallel path he made muffled pig noises. They bolted, and he had to yell to reassure them. They refused to look at him for the rest of the day, though would occasionally burst into slightly hysterical shrieks of laughter.

The watercourse is in limestone country and has eroded the limestone into isolated cliffs and islands, with red sand dunes on the eastern side. If I had a more reliable vehicle I would attempt to follow it down to the beginning of the salt lakes. My father did it once and said it was like coming upon the end of the world, or its beginning. I am still following his voice.

Or maybe it is another voice and my father heard it too, the voice of a mysterious stranger who rides at the periphery of the mapmaker's tale. His name is Chance, or Luck, or Risk, and the mapmaker speaks of him with ambivalence, even distrust. He shadows her journey as she shadows mine.

> *Chance speaks even less than before. He rides beside me like an apparition. When he turns towards me I can no longer see his face. Sometimes I feel as if he is another part of myself, my cast shadow moving always a little ahead of me, inseparable from me yet always out of reach. His presence is not reassuring, merely inevitable.*

The lakes pull me like a magnet. Maybe next trip (except that I am not coming back). Maybe in the heart of white Australia is a dried-up salt lake and a dream of redemption, tempered with irony.

⁂

TODAY I TRAVEL WITH MALLEY to the place we know of as Mt Phyllis, and the rockholes of Lorna Springs. These names, given by the stock-route party after the wives of Bill Wilson and Milton Willick, are no longer in common usage, and I do not know the Aboriginal names.

Reading Davidson's description of the Tanami rockholes, I think at first that he is describing Lorna Springs.

> Camp 66. Thursday, August 9th, 1900.
> The rockholes were a splendid sight, being situated in the

roughest part of the gorge. They were surrounded by high precipitous rocks, and over both water was still running. They were situated on different levels ... The upper was heart-shaped, wide, and ten feet in depth ... The lower hole was circular, somewhat smaller in appearance, but of greater depth ... The measurement of this hole gave 20 000 galls. of clear crystal rainwater. The unfortunate part about these holes was that they were practically inaccessible to stock.

Lorna Springs is in a long low red escarpment. The approach to the gorge is much rougher and stonier than I remember. The gorge and the rockholes are the same. I first saw this place with my father. We made the short climb to the rockholes while the Aboriginal stockmen remained at the entrance. Whether they were reluctant to go in I do not remember. They did not seem to know much about the place, although it must have been extremely significant as a rare permanent water supply. But this was not their country, most of them came from Billiluna and further west. On the other hand, maybe they just weren't telling.

The first rockhole is perfectly circular, almost three metres across. It is undercut beneath the rim, and when the water level is low, birds and creatures fall in and cannot get out. Once my father rescued a wedge-tailed eagle, which watched him with unblinking yellow eyes, heaving its sodden wings when it felt the lasso of aerial wire fall across them. As a young man Malley attempted to measure its depth, diving in and striking a current some metres below the surface. He came up fast, imagining himself swept into the wet red darkness, drowning while just above the sun shone on bright rock.

Overlooking the waterhole, a little way up the gorge wall, is a large boulder. The shelf behind it is sandy and smooth.

When I came here the first time there was a pile of round stones conveniently placed for a crouching hunter to hurl at an unwary wallaby coming to drink. Faded ochre hieroglyphs made soft patterns on the rock, barely visible until the eye learned where to look.

Higher up is the second, triangular hole. On the day I came with my father it held a shallow pool of stained water and was thick with brown and orange butterflies. Today it is dry, as are the waterholes along the creeks.

The second time I came here with Malley, en route to Billiluna. We met a mechanic travelling back to the Territory from the mission, who insisted on coming in to look at the rockholes. His attitude towards me was avuncular and sentimental. I did not trust such cloying regard, having seen it too often in violent men. It outraged me that such a person should invite himself into this place. It outraged me that I should attract this unwelcome regard merely because I was young and female. Remembering, I grin a little wryly to myself. These days the mechanic wouldn't give me a second glance.

This time it is the paintings which hold my attention. Some at least have been retouched recently. The genius loci, a red snake, undulates across a shelf of rock above the circle of water. The ochre is matt and fresh. I pay homage to the old spirit in his new skin, crawling forever on the rock face. The pile of stones behind the boulder has gone. It is afternoon and the gorge is in shadow. It is easy to feel mysterious affinities with the energies and presences in such a place. Not so easy to feel them for the real people, who live here still. The past is more tractable than the present, being less cluttered with contradictions. As we leave, Malley remarks that a pile of flat stones near the entrance to the gorge may be a grave. He throws away these snippets of knowledge. I do not ask him how he knows. I have never asked him about the Aboriginal part of his heritage. If I did so now, he would be surprised and embarrassed.

17

A LARGE BLACK BLOTCH TURNS the border section on Davidson's map into terra nullius. He travelled from the north-east, crossing briefly into Western Australia at the intersection of the 129th north-south and the 20th east-west parallels, and headed towards the southern end of the Lewis Range. The section of the diary I have begins at this point, in Western Australia, at camps 53 and 54. The quality of the photocopying is very bad, the print blurred and difficult to read. He crosses back into the Territory more or less where the present road cuts the border, and where the stock-route land party crossed on the return leg of their journey.

Camp 55. Wednesday, July 25th, 1900.
We sighted a somewhat prominent flat-topped hill on a continuation of our bearings. I decided to steer for the flat-topped hill with the double object of seeing if there was anything along the flanks of the far range, and also of examining the country in the vicinity of the flat-topped hill.

I am confused by Davidson's references to the flat-topped hill. It seems probable that he is referring to Mt Tracey, but I can't make the map and diary references tally. My father has pencilled in the location on Davidson's map, and it is not on the line between camps 55 and 56. I follow my nose, cutting south along station tracks until I can see the sandstone hill, then leave the track and drive across the flat grasslands to its foot.

I climb the steep slope of broken sandstone and look for Davidson's name scratched on a rock at the summit. *Davidson, 1900.* I remember it clearly. Bruce Farrands, my brother and I climbed Mt Tracey one afternoon, and we found his name and the year scratched at the base of a cairn of stones. But today I can't find it. I begin to wonder whether I imagined it. Until this moment I would have sworn to the memory. I can recall the quality of the air of that particular afternoon. It must have been winter because it was mild and the shadows were barely beginning to stretch towards the middle of the afternoon. But I am no longer confident of the things my mind conjures up.

I stand on Mt Tracey and the Davidson party weaves its slow progress across the landscape, a line of camels, five men and the shadowy presence of a small dog. Davidson's journal describes the surrounding country and the view from the summit. It is not much changed, though in this dry time there is little evidence of bird life, and the 'splendid grass flats' are grazed to a blond stubble.

> Camp 57. Friday, July 27th, 1900.
> I obtained a good view from the summit of the hill, which was surrounded by open grass flats. To the south-west and west were several short tablelands extending round to the end of the detached range. Blackfellow's

smokes were visible in this direction, and also to the northward beyond a strong depression which encircled the grass country . . .

Birds were extremely numerous about this locality, and coming along early this morning, with splendid grass flats to walk on, flocks of grass parrots and birds of other description chirping and singing, made me for a while imagine I was in a more favoured locality than Central Australia.

The hill on which I stand is the most striking feature in this part of the country. It is named after my sister, whose life has been as touched and troubled by this place as my own, though in a different way. Her child's footprints make small smudges, a part of the pattern of women's tracks across the country. There are many tracks, my mother, my sister, the girl I was, Daisy and Millie and Margaret and Patricia, all the women who travelled this way, the ancestral women and the ones who have come back to their country.

My adult feet, bare and white and bony, toenails painted a brave red, search for the right path. It is like a tentative and stumbling dance, stepping as lightly as possible in order to displace nothing and to avoid doing myself an injury. There is a big story here, about women and country, too big for me to tell. Or maybe it is not a big story but many small stories, spreading in intricate detail across the country. They are barely visible beneath the more emphatic stories of exploration and development. Those are the big stories, but they no longer convince us as they used to. They need to be amended and retold, the possibilities teased out towards different endings.

The Suzuki looks tiny and far away. The hill is not particularly high, but it is a curious feature of this country that any change of perspective is exaggerated. The tyre marks show clearly on the ironstone pebbles they have displaced. This gives me an idea, to make a mark or a sign, like the hieroglyphs in the Chilean desert. A whirlwind appears on the horizon, a cone of red dust manifesting like an ancestral spirit. It hangs there, undulating slightly. As I climb down over the sharp red flakes of stone a small wind rushes suddenly past my feet like an escaping animal. As a child I took it for granted that the country communicated through the elements, and through trees and stones and creatures. So it still feels to me, though I can no longer take it for granted.

I walk a circle on the ironstone flat, my footprints slowly dislodging the polished reddish-black pebbles, revealing the paler earth beneath them. It takes a while. Step by step I engrave a circle at the foot of the flat-topped hill which bears my sister's name. I cannot tell whether I am completing something or simply describing the process of covering the same ground, trapped in the self-contained story of my own past. I climb the hill again to see how it looks. It is clearly visible. I wonder how long it will remain.

In the narrow shade of the Suzuki I fill in my journal, the pen scratching its mundane notations of days and events and locations. It is all I can do, to record my movements, describe the country, hope that this net of words will catch something which I cannot articulate.

18

I TRAVEL EAST, THEN NORTH, then east again, tracking Davidson. This gives me a superficial sense of purpose, and staves off the sense of being on a fool's mission. A set of wheel tracks, disused, cuts north from the main track. I know without recourse to my maps that it must lead to Macfarlane's Bore. It is odd how familiar it all feels, after so long, as if my body has stored the information. Partly it is a picture, a mental image of tracks and locations, but it is something else too, a set of visceral alignments over which the intellect has no jurisdiction.

A mile or two along the spinifex-muffled track I find the bore, which is overgrown and abandoned. The column and tanks have rusted out from the salty water. Just north of the bore a line of low sandstone hills breaks the profile of the horizon. Davidson's route took him through this point, travelling in a north-easterly direction from landmark to landmark. I make the short rough climb to the top of the nearest hill and look out towards the pinnacle hills and tableland of Davidson's journal. The view has not changed.

Sunday, July 29th, 1900.
From the summit of these hills the surrounding country was visible for a considerable distance, showing some likely looking pinnacle hills six miles distant to the north-east, with a strong tableland range beyond to the east of this line at about eleven miles.

Inscribed in the language of a surveyor, Davidson's story is still visible in landforms and foliage and horizon lines, but it belongs to a particular time. Bits of the Davidson journey have disappeared. It was in this rough escarpment that his sidekick Byrne discovered a rockhole fed by a small waterfall and overhung with figtrees. My father searched in vain for this rockhole and, in spite of the specific description of its location, never found it. Of course I cannot resist searching for it, without success. Some time between 1900 and 1963 the figtree rockhole ceased to exist. The people disappeared as well. By the time my father came into the country there were traces and relics, but the dreaming track which traversed that part of the country had become a story lodged in the mind of its custodians, who had gone away. The rockhole is like the place in the Borges story which is kept in existence by the visits of a horse. Eventually the horse dies and nobody comes there any more, and the place is forgotten, then one day it is simply not there any more. First the people went away from the rockhole. Then the big animals forgot it, and the birds, and last of all the lizards and hopping mice and butterflies. By the time my father read the Davidson journal and went looking for it, the rockhole had slipped out of memory and out of existence.

The country north of Macfarlane's showed all the signs of gold-bearing country. Again and again Davidson's journal records raised hopes of discovering traces of gold; again and again the samples prove disappointing.

Camp No 61. Saturday, August 4th, 1900.
The panning off of all our choice samples confirmed the work of yesterday, inasmuch as every sample panned showed a clean dish—not even a microscopical colour being visible. Anywhere else this result obtained from such splendid reefs traversing good metalliferous country would be considered extraordinary. Here it was what we were learning to expect.

Davidson's geological instinct has since been vindicated. Rich goldmines have been opened in recent times in the country he explored. But the best gold stories, the ones I believe in, are the stories in which gold is found and lost again.

One of our stock-camp cooks told of an uncle of his who found a gold reef somewhere to the south-west. He loaded samples of gold into the pack and set out for civilisation. But the packhorse died, and the uncle had to jettison most of the gold, along with a bag of horseshoes, in order to lighten the load on the horse he was riding. He was never able to locate the spot again. So somewhere out there, on an ironstone ridge, there is a bag of rusting horseshoes, the bones of a packhorse and a pack full of gold nuggets.

There is another story, told to us by a traveller with a broken-down ute and a wild look in his eye. He was searching for the bones of a duck. Where were these bones supposed to be located, we asked him. On the edge of a claypan somewhere to the east of here, he told us. An uncle of his (uncles seem to be an essential part of the story) found gold and nearly died, only saving himself by catching a wild duck on a claypan full of water. His relative ate the duck raw and left the bones, so the traveller told us, and if he could just find those duck bones he would be well on the way to finding the gold. We asked him how long ago all this had taken place, and he said thirty, maybe forty years. We asked him how, if he found the bones, he would be sure they belonged to the right duck, and he said he would know by instinct.

Technology has taken the myth out of the search for gold. Today, once reefs have been found they stay found. But out there somewhere a packsaddle rots on an ironstone ridge and the forty-year-old bones of a duck leave traces of gold in the imagination.

As for the man Davidson, what do I know about him? He did not get lost or die, so there is no folklore or mythology surrounding him. He was too competent to capture the imagination of history. The little information I have is contradictory. For years all I had was the diary excerpt, copied from the South Australian Lands Department Archives. The date is clearly 1900, and there seemed no reason to doubt that this was when his survey took place. When I searched for more information all I could find was an entry in the *Australian Biographical Dictionary*, giving his date of birth as 1878 and the Tanami expedition as circa 1909. In 1900 he would have been twenty-two years old.

So I am left with a double exposure, a cheerful turn of the century young man and his older, steadier counterpart of 1909. They move companionably through my story, usually walking beside their camels, in the company of second-in-command Byrne, the enigmatic Pater and the shadowy Woods, and the Aboriginal boy, Jack. The young surveyor was commissioned by the Central Exploration Syndicate to equip and lead the 'Western Expedition' out from Barrow Creek to the West Australian border. The expedition was a geological survey to look for gold, and although Davidson found evidence of gold, and more importantly permanent water supplies at the Granites and Tanami, his assessment of both sites was that their remoteness and the lack of major reefs made development at that time uneconomical. In spite of his advice, mines were established at both sites, but the inaccessibility, lack of water and harsh conditions defeated all but the most determined and experienced prospectors. There was a brief and abortive rush at the Granites in 1932, and limited mining continued until the early 1950s, after which the mines were abandoned until the 1980s when new technology made them viable once again.

In the opening lines of his journal Davidson remarks:

> The exploration and development of Central Australia is a history of hardships and disappointments, and our experience, covering three of the driest years ever recorded in that country, was no exception.

The assumption is that an expedition that does not find either mineral wealth or pastoral country is a failure. If there is a streak of romanticism in Allan Davidson, it is well concealed. He has a job to do and does it with remarkable authority. The voice of the journal is pragmatic, scientific, detailed and thorough. It is articulate, sometimes discursive and even humorous. There is in the language an awareness that this is a document which will be read by others, a document of exploration and potentially significant discovery. What was the world Allan Arthur Davidson travelled through at the beginning of a new century? Australia was on the brink of

Federation. The promise for settlement and progress was in the notion of mineral wealth, which it was believed would transform the desolate waste of Central Australia into a place of prosperity. Spencer and Gillen had embarked on their collaborative study of the native tribes of Central Australia. Ethnographers around the world were excited by the prospect of information regarding a people who appeared to be living a Stone-Age existence. The hint of an awareness of the cultural complexity of indigenous Australians was beginning to infiltrate Australian society.

Davidson's only direct encounter with the Aborigines of the Tanami occurred near the Tanami rockholes. It is worth quoting for the glimpse it gives of the curiosity, wariness and opportunism each party brought to the encounter.

> Camp 66. Sunday, August 12th, 1900.
> Jack sighted three blackfellows at the rockholes, and induced them to come and pay their respects to the camp. The party consisted of one old man and two young men. The former was very doubtful of the advisability of coming too close, and stood on top of the range to wait the reception accorded the others. When he saw that they were given a feed, he concluded it was safe, and joined them. They were about the average height, but somewhat bony and weedy. On enquiry, the boy learned that the native name of the rockhole was 'Tanami', and that they never 'died'—the conclusion we had already formed. They were shown the gold specimens, but had never seen anything like it before ... They knew where the stone came from, and volunteered the information that there was 'mobs' of similar stone to the east, together with a large creek containing plenty of water and fish.

Monday, August 13th, 1900
The natives fulfilled their promise, and paid the camp another visit. One of the younger was replaced by a stranger, who was deeply interested in things generally. No fresh information was gleaned from them. On leaving our visitors incidentally took along with them a quartpot which was lying at the waterhole, so we shall probably not see them again.

Davidson was more than usually interested in Aboriginal society, citing Spencer and Gillen, and making reference to the tribal divisions as being similar to those of 'the Great Arunta Tribe'. He noted extensive evidence of the trading of iron tomahawks into the region, in spite of lack of contact with whites, and described the hitherto unrecorded customs of weaving spinifex capes and sand-thatching the bough shelters. However, his observations in the journal are usually to do with the sightings of smoke and tracks and the reliance of the party on this evidence to locate soaks and rockholes. The dependence on Aboriginal knowledge to locate water is a recurring motif in the exploration of Australian deserts. In his crossing of the Great Sandy Desert, gentleman explorer David Carnegie habitually captured and tied up lone Aborigines, forcing them to lead his party to water, and on one occasion feeding the captive salt beef to make him thirsty. Davidson, however, was generally successful in his use of smoke signals, which were answered by any Aborigines in the vicinity. There is a somewhat poignant entry when the camels had gone some nine days without water, and the party pursued what it believed to be answering smokes, only to discover them to be whirlwinds rising from the ash of freshly burned country. It was here too, in the region of the Smoke Hills, that mirage distorted the landscape 'into snow-topped mountains instead of wretched little hills', making it impossible to take accurate bearings. I have seen this phenomenon myself, in the late winter when unseasonal humidity invades the atmosphere. It is an odd experience, to see a familiar place take flight into the regions of fantasy.

19

When I first attempted to read Davidson's diary I found it impossibly dry. I wanted to read a tale of adventure, loss, frustrated desire. I wanted something that Gosse or Giles might have written, not a pedestrian document about travertine limestone, camel feed and dollied samples. But each time I read it now it draws me in a little further. Between the lines, through the geological terminology and the practical daily accounts of camps and landforms, a young man of twenty-two, with his small band of men and camels, pursues the chimaeras of gold and smoke and water. The small dog which began the expedition with them was lost somewhere near the nonexistent 'High Mountain Ranges', victim of some dog-chimaera of its own: 'Our dog rushed out barking into the night and disappeared for good.'

Wretched little hills turn into snow-capped peaks, and native smokes are discovered to be whirlwinds of ash. The few features marked on the map prove to be in the wrong place and misleadingly described. Everywhere the country promises the signs of gold and delivers nothing. The other human inhabitants of the country are rarely sighted, the traces of their presence evidenced by tracks, abandoned campsites and the marks of burning. Watercourses run so infrequently that it is impossible to tell the direction of the flow of water. Ancient marshlands and dried-up claypans hint at the remnants of great systems of inland lakes, the inland sea which runs like a thread through the Australian psyche.

In a lecture given to the Adelaide Geographical Society in about 1902, Charles Winneke says of the Davidson expedition:

> 'The journey, owing to his able management, was a thorough success. No mishaps of any kind occurred, and Mr Davidson has assured me that the utmost harmony prevailed throughout the party during their long and tedious journey. I consider Mr Davidson's journey, although not quite so extensive, should be classed with that of other leading explorers; his work is of double interest also to us by the fact that it gives us a correct knowledge of the topographical as well as geological nature of the country, which has not been the case with many other explorers, and I feel certain that his traverse is more than ordinarily accurate. Mr Davidson's work covers 27 000 square miles, and fills up one of the blank spaces in the map of Australia ...'

Thorough, painstaking and competent, Davidson too has almost slipped from memory. His rivers, unlike Mitchell's mythical river to India, flow nowhere. His inland sea is a dried-up marshland disappearing under sand dunes. Even the timing of his expedition has become misplaced in the records of Australian exploration.

He comes through the poorly photocopied and fading pages as practical and good-humoured. Did he question himself, doubt his ability as leader of the expedition? Did he feel the strangeness and the silence of the country through which he travelled? Several pages of the diary copy are impossible to decipher, so I sit in the shade cast by the rusting tanks and try to unearth the unwritten diary that is concealed in the blurred print.

> Three months into the journey, and as yet we have not found gold-bearing country. The type of country is unfamiliar, and I lose confidence in my ability to read it. The strangeness of it affects us all in a different fashion; Byrne becomes more noncommittal, Woods by turn morose and garrulous, and the Pater more eccentric and unreliable. The boy, who by all accounts one would expect to be most at home in this setting, exhibits a growing uneasiness. I put this down to the naturally timid and superstitious nature of the blackfellow when faced with the unfamiliar.
>
> We travel through a monotony of landscape, in which were I not obliged to take bearings, find camel feed and water, in other words to take care of the daily requirements of the expedition, I might easily lose my bearings and my sense of purpose. As leader I can let no glimpse of this become visible to the other members of the party, although there are times when I suspect Byrne has some intimation of it, being a perceptive fellow, though not communicative. This may be purely conjecture on my part, a need to impute to a companion the possibility of some fellow feeling. One becomes aware of one's fundamental isolation in these circumstances.
>
> The country itself exerts a presence which causes one to question one's most firmly held suppositions. There is a point in each day when purpose and will threaten to

evaporate, and one feels oneself travelling in an aimless hallucination of sunlight and silence.

This Davidson satisfies my desire for self-questioning, my contemporary need for a glimpse of the inner man. But he would never have written it. He was twenty-two years old, maybe; a nineteenth-century man. Could he have questioned the exploitation of the country for gold or pastoral purposes? I do not think so. It was not in the vocabulary of the time.

Sixty years later my father's diary tells nothing of the mysteries that moved him and the fears that haunted him. Any faint whispers questioning pastoral practices are simply echos of the eccentric noise of cranks and fools. And yet I know it would hurt my father at a very deep level to see the country now and to know that he was in part responsible for its domestication. He never wanted to come back and see this country again. On the occasions when someone visited with news of it, he would rather not have listened. He sometimes indicated a regret that the country had ever been developed, and he would have been happy enough to see it revert to wilderness. He received the news that it had become an Aboriginal station with equanimity. I think secretly he preferred the Aborigines to have it. He was a queer mixture of conventional attitudes to land development and an almost mystical belief in the redemptive power of the land. He loved the country for its remoteness and inaccessibility, yet spent years of his life developing it and bringing it under control. He was both a practical man and a dreamer, and the two cohabited uneasily. I think the older he got, the more he felt the contradictions of his position.

DAVIDSON HAS PROVIDED ME with a brief reprieve from my real purpose. The rusting tanks, the immobilised windmill of Macfarlane's Bore stand as a harsh memorial to the failures and endeavours of my father's time. This bore was the northernmost watering point on the lease, the site where my father encountered a bewildered road gang from Western Australia, hoodwinked by Father on Balgo into believing they were grading a track on mission territory. Father's plan was to subvert passing traffic to bypass the mission, sending travellers instead through the back roads and bore runs of Mongrel Downs. My father, enraged, drove the grader gang off at gunpoint, though they went readily enough when they realised they were twenty miles inside the Northern Territory border.

It was here too that my father spotted tracks of a mob of horses travelling west, some of them shod, and put together fragments of rumour, of horses gone missing on properties far to the north and east. He guessed who the horse thieves were. Hydraulic and Trewalla had established themselves on a block to the north and were old hands at subsidising their various enterprises. He guessed too where the horses had gone and quietly indicated his suspicions to Father, though not in so many words. The border war went quiet for a while, since it wouldn't do for a Catholic priest to be suspected of receiving stolen horses.

SAM POKES ABOUT HAPPILY among the ruins, sniffing and peeing, bringing his dog's perspective to this site of ancient dramas. Any dingo that strays into this place is going to know that Sam the Dog was here. I make a small fire and put the billy on to boil, spread a slice of damper with jam and think about what to do next. I have no plan, just a desire to move from one location to another, to absorb a sense of the country, to remember. There is a relief in being alone, after the tough confronting energy of the women's business and the uneasiness of encounters with old friends.

I could not articulate what brought me back here, except that I was afraid. Since I was a child who had to climb the narrow ladder to the top of the overhead tank, I have understood that there is something important on the other side of fear. It is not courage which pushes me towards it. It is more akin to what I remember of my mother's driving technique when she encountered a bad stretch of sand or mud. She would aim the vehicle in the right direction, shut her eyes and put her foot down. After a few experiences of being in the car with her on these occasions, we children would insist on being let out to walk, leaving her to make the blind dash alone.

The point is, one does not stop being afraid. I am making my own blind, fearful dash, with no idea of where I will find myself when I open my eyes.

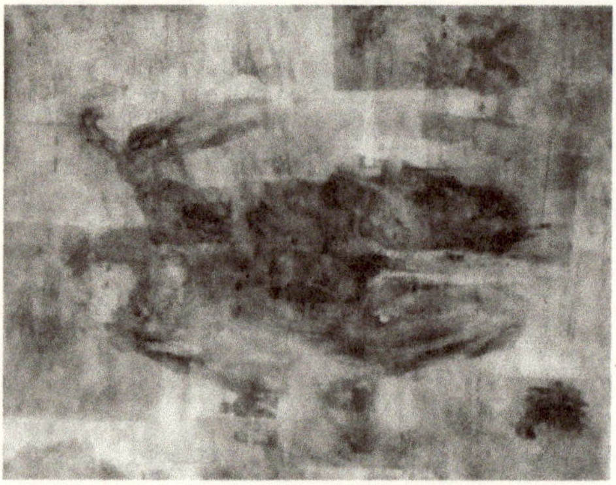

20

WHEN I TOLD MY MOTHER I was coming back to this country she said to me—Take some of Joe's ashes with you. Part of him always belonged out there.

It was a generous suggestion, because she knew the part of him which always eluded her belonged here. Prising open the rosewood box of ashes was a little like digging up a grave. My mother hid in the living room while I did it. I found an empty tea container, a brand he always liked, and transferred a portion of the ashes into it. They have given me less discomfort than my memories. I can deal with concrete things, but ghosts give me trouble. Although I did not make my journey in order to scatter my father's ashes, the tea tin has been on my mind. I know the place, I think, but I will not be certain until I am there.

We called it Bullock's Head Lake. It is shaped like the elongated head of a bullock, with the horns formed by two creeks at its western end. The last time I was here was with my father, and the lake was full of water. It is not really a lake, but an immense shallow claypan which has been intermittently filling and drying back for millennia. We came over the rise and there it was, this tremendous expanse of water, remote and self-contained. Waterfowl scurried into the shallows, the boree shadowed the rim like a fortress. To the south-west a long red dune lay sheltered by sprawling ti-tree, its surface scattered with flints and grinding stones, so numerous that the place must have served as a seasonal campsite for a very long time.

It has not changed. It is dry, marked and powdered with cattle tracks, but the same. Still, remote and silent. I find firewood in a stand of boree, but make camp in the open, close to the lake's edge. It is nearly sundown, the country all about me luminous with that saturated colour which seems to come from the earth itself, as if I could take a handful of it and see it gleam gently with its own interior fire. Although this place is full of memories, it is clear to me that my father no longer belongs here. If I leave the ashes, it is for myself, and for the country, not for him.

⁂

THE GIRL SITS NEAR HER father, the campfire burning between them. The sun is going out on the western horizon. She is barely a child any more, on the brink of adolescence and resisting it fiercely. If there is a way to avoid becoming an adult, she will find it. But at this moment she is focused with perfect intensity on her father's words. They glow and burn in the ardent heart of the child, whose whole being leans towards the man and his words. She wants nothing more than to perfect her capacity to listen and respond. He speaks about the country, and she knows the words before they are spoken, because they seem to come from inside herself. This fierce love she feels encompasses her father and the night sky and the deepening red curve of the land, a landscape which might appear nondescript but to her is full of subtlety and nuance, because here in the beam of her father's love and approval her soul comes fiercely to life. She would walk out into the desert and die with him without a backward glance. She would walk out and die alone if he thought it was necessary.

I look back in wonder at this child who feels so intensely, so absolutely, and am almost regretful that I can only remember how it was, that pure unquestioning intensity of feeling, particularly in the light of all I have since felt about my father and about this country. If love can purify or save, the love the girl feels is of that order. The country is illuminated by that beam of love. It is her father's country, and what he loves, she loves.

I cannot see my father clearly. My own sense of who I wanted to be was so closely bound up with his approval that it has created a kind of tunnel vision. He is framed distantly within a circle of light, and I can't see beyond it. What I begin to understand is that my real difficulties with my father do not belong to this place. Those childhood years, intense and vivid, are illuminated with a vast unboundaried passion to protect and preserve the magic circle of my family and home. They are haunted by an intermittent melody of fear and pain, which intensifies as my father's drinking reaches crisis point. But the crisis is averted, the world does not come apart. The adventure of our lives remains intact, and so does my father the hero.

After we moved to Queensland the legacy of my double life began to manifest itself. I continued to put in my time, returning at every opportunity from university, from travelling, from the slow formulation of my career as an artist, to help out and to offer support. I did not resent this, in fact I continued to draw much of my sense of identity from this link to land and family. But my father's world was narrowing as my own broadened. The only point of intersection was in my return visits, and it became increasingly difficult to describe or share any but the most superficial aspects of my life. And I had no real desire to do more than that. I could see no point in precipitating the silent withdrawal that was my father's normal response to attitudes of which he disapproved. But I felt over the years the slow erosion of honesty from the relationship, and this caused a kind of pain from which it seems there is no recovery. I think my father's power over me always lay in his vulnerability, and the fact that my own reflected his too closely. I can take no credit for the care with which I nurtured the remnants of our relationship. Should he have broken, I feared as much for myself as for him.

Can it be that I have come back not to lay my father's ghost but to recover something of the man to whom I gave such unconditional childish allegiance? To offer him a simpler grief, as unconditional as that child's love. If so, I have not succeeded. The man who was here continues to elude me, and I am left with the burden of my adult grief, shapeless and incomplete.

THIS MORNING I WAKE BEFORE daylight. The fire is still smouldering, so I throw on some wood before drifting back into a light sleep. Suddenly it is first light and I am sharply awake. The smoke from the fire has spread across the lake and weaves into the ti-tree on the far shore, more than a kilometre away. I collect the container with my father's ashes and am up and following the path of smoke onto the lake bed before I have had time to think. This is the time and place. I walk far out onto the lake surface, the smoke curling and drifting around my knees. I am wading knee-deep in smoke. On the lake bed bizarre small succulent flowers grow, which look like something you might find growing on the surface of Mars. Towards the middle of the lake I open the container and shake the ashes into my palm. They are gritty, more like holding a handful of fine gravel than the soft feathery wood ash with which I am familiar. So this is what is left of a man. This is my father's material remains, cupped in the palm of my hands. Of itself it has no meaning, beyond what I choose to invest in it. My father's spirit departed a long time ago. This is a symbol for me to use for my own purpose. I scatter the ash carefully in a circle around me and then step outside it. But it seems too final, too complete. Such things are not ended so easily. I kneel and scrape a break in the circle's perimeter and place the tiny portion of ash and dried clay back in the container. The grief I feel has little to do with my father. It is for loss and time and the remote familiar contours of sand dune and ti-tree and boree. The profile of the far shore with its garland of smoke matches a template of recognition, as if it was here, in this place, that some ancestor stood upright, looked forward and saw a pattern of shapes which were inscribed forever behind the eyes. It feels right, to have made this offering of my father's substance, for it to become part of the lake surface and to seep into it with the next rain. This tracing of his life onto the lake surface joins the passages of millennia. One more passing of a life, no more or less significant than the dying back of trees and grasses, the broken egg of a mallee fowl, the crumbling away of a plateau, the ebbing of an inland sea.

BACK AT THE FIRE, SAM is uncomfortable. He does not like these overt expressions of emotion. I put the coffee on to brew and watch the smoke rise off the lake, thinking about nothing at all.

I am not ready to leave. I lay out the groundsheet and my box of ochres and pigments. The centre of the groundsheet is a dark rectangle, gridded to resemble a map. Somewhere within the boundaries of the dark space is the point of reference for which I am searching. I feel angry, full of wild physical unease, suffocated by memories and maps and history. I want to be here, now, without memory, without a past, without prior knowledge of this place. I want my life and my presence to be as meaningless and integral to the place as the pale dusty clay and the smoke and the debris of leaf and bark. I take handfuls of ash from the campfire and mix them into a paste in the camp oven. With the paste I mark out a circle which cuts through the edges of the dark rectangle. Then I find my cache of red ochre and mix it into the ash until the paste is a gritty deep red. I strip off my clothes, plaster my body with the mess of ash and ochre, and print it onto the black space, again and again. The prints come up like red bones.

The morning shifts through noon into the unassailable space of the afternoon. The dried ochre and ash itches and flakes. My body registers a breathless, spasmodic tension. If I remain very still I am able to let the surges of energy pass without collapsing into the rage and panic which seem to be at the source of it. This impossible country, which leaves one stupefied with emptiness. It recedes and recedes beyond my grasp. At the same time it takes hold of me at the very centre and wrings me slowly and excrutiatingly with a need and a desire which I cannot even identify, let alone assuage. People talk with such facility of its spirituality, but I have no idea what they mean. What I am feeling is physical, almost sexual. I want to scrape my flesh against the ragged bark of the boree, draw blood, crawl naked into the blinding stillness of the lake surface. So much Aboriginal myth and ritual is pervaded by a harsh sexuality. Genitals are slashed or penetrated with stones. The primordial landscape is scattered with the evidence of ancestral acts of rape, copulation, dismembering. It is about a physical encounter with the land itself, a wounding, a letting of blood, a taking of the country into oneself, of taking oneself into the country.

Many of the whites who live here struggle to articulate an attachment over which they have no control. They leave and return, resentfully, full of anger and indigestible griefs. The hard arid contours of the landscape become synonymous with the failures of will and desire that have driven them away and compelled them to return. What price the homage this country extracts? Acceptance, predicated on limited ambition; a moment by moment focus on the job to be done, the life to be lived. Seen at close quarters it is unendurable, but at the same time contains a narrow and deeply grounded wisdom. I would give anything for that sort of wisdom, not to be torn with ambiguities. But that is not true, of course. One never truly wishes to give up knowledge, whatever the cost.

The stillness of this immense dry lake is unimaginable. It is as if all the silence that is the measure of this country is distilled in this place, into something for which there are no words. The movement of my breathing, the beating of my heart, violates it. I lie wrapped in the groundsheet, scarcely breathing, chilled in spite of the sun.

Today I fell down on the lake, and did not wake for many hours. I dreamed that it stretched to the horizon in all directions. I was alone, and the surface on which I walked was made up of the bones and feathers and fur of creatures. Across this blighted landscape a figure approached, and as it came nearer I was afraid, for I recognised myself, walking inwards from the blind horizon. I turned to avoid this meeting, gripped in the helpless lethargy of dreams, and saw the same figure approaching from the way I had come. I turned and turned, and from every direction the figure came inexorably on, a crowding apparition from which there was no escape.

I hold off the mapmaker's phantoms with an act of will. The place she invites me to share is too austere, these glimpses too deep for my imagination to follow. Washing off the ash and ochre shifts me back into my own skin. I do not want to think too much about all this. The shadows begin to move across the lake surface, cast by the small mad plants which grow on it. I am anxious for familiar human contact. As I drive away the stillness reaches out behind me. My past is dissolving as I touch it, each place and moment insisting on its own present.

You can never step into the same river twice.

Much quoted Heraclitus. But I have stepped into the dry space of an inland lake.

21

FROM BULLOCK'S HEAD LAKE I take the shortest route to the Tanami Downs homestead, a courtesy visit to let the manager and his wife know my movements. The normality of the small family group at the homestead is almost surreal. They have been generous and hospitable, have not questioned my desire to drive about the country alone. They have taken for granted that I know my way about, that my credentials for being here are legitimate. I feel I should be able to present them with some landscape sketches, something traditional and familiar, as evidence of my good faith as an artist. But I have nothing suitable, explainable, to offer. The groundsheet would hardly be appropriate. To describe what I actually do as an artist would be as difficult as explaining the real purpose of my journey. The imposter quietly steps in, talks in the vernacular of the country of cattle and drought and changes. I listen with bemusement, almost impressed by this chameleon creature which shares my skin, which only hours ago was coated in ochre and ash.

BACK AT LAKE RUTH. I HAVE spent a quiet day here and feel myself slowly taking hold of it, and it of me. Just being here does it, spending time and paying attention. In this place in particular I can feel a part of myself that is still deeply aligned to this country. There is pleasure in making camp, the familiar ritual of setting up my small table, collecting firewood, boiling the billy, planning my evening meal of rice and tuna and the few remaining fresh vegetables. My camp is orderly and spartan. It suits me, to have the necessities of life contained in the back of a ute. For a brief time I can indulge the fantasy of a simplified ascetic life, free of attachments and the messy demands of relationships and responsibilities.

I drag the up-ended boat onto the groundsheet and draw around it. Shield-shaped, heraldic, it cuts the edges of the mapped rectangle. Sam wanders about through wet pigments, leaving paw prints, as if a lion has walked across the shield.

Later I walk across the brittle white surface of the lake to the far side. There was a portent of my father's death engraved here, erased now by time and water, a hundred-metre channel scored by the nose of a light plane attempting to land. I imagine the shape of the aircraft, a broken silver cross impressed into the white circle of the claypan. My father's diary entry describing the crash is non-commital.

> Station diary. Friday, 1st November, 1963.
> Departed in plane approx. 12.30 pm and followed the stock route looking for Litchie. Flew over Ferdie's camp. Plane crashed at Lake Ruth.
> Shaken up and Bill got cut over his eye and was out to it for several hours.
> Had the little portable with us and the plane battery was still OK.

> Plane upside down. Got on to the Alice Springs base about 2.30 and arrangements made for rescue.
> Our main trouble no water. Walked back to the Homestead bore that night and I had my first drink of water from the future Mahood home. It looked and tasted like nectar in the moonlight.
> Bore had been equipped only a few days.

This is one of my father's voices, the practical, unembellished voice, with that one lapse into poetic cliché. The man it conjures up was here, in this place. He is far more convincing than the phantom I am pursuing across a landscape I have invented.

As light plane accidents go, this one was remarkably well orchestrated. They crashed on a clearly defined landmark. The radio and battery were operative. The crash was caused by a faulty fuel cap which allowed the fuel to vaporise, so there was no fire after impact. They were within four miles of water. The rescue was organised within a few hours, injuries were minor, mostly concussion and shock. My father's diary entries give no indication of the fear and panic as the plane went down. I remember him describing the scramble to get out, still afraid of fire, and of Bill Waudby ripping the door off the plane with adrenalin-charged strength in order to pull out Bill Wilson, who was unconscious. Someone walked the two miles to retrieve the storpedo dropped by the rescue plane. When they opened it it contained no water, but quantities of toilet paper. The laconic voice of the diary describes the arrival of the rescue party the day after the crash, and the four hundred mile journey to Alice Springs over a bush track.

> Ground party arrived with a load of tucker and grog.
> Didn't feel like any of it.

Long hot trip back and at one stage we all flaked out on side of road.
Two punctures and rough.

I don't remember any drama being attached to the news of the crash. Everyone was safe, to my child's eye view it was no big deal. I don't even remember extracting any prestige from it at school.

Nine years of my family's history are layered into this lake surface, dry and dusty now, intermittently filling and drying in the years we lived here, sometimes a clear blue expanse, sometimes a shallow milky puddle, always a focus for us. They are like palimpsests, these inland lakes. Everything drains into them from the surrounding country, everything is distilled into a tracing of events and passages, erased and reinscribed and erased. This one is an important site, a red ochre place in the dreamtime. Did the tear the plane made on the skin of the lake set loose some angry spirit, and has my father's death appeased it?

Walking out on the lake surface I carry my father's death with me. No, it is his life I carry. I believed that his death freed me, as the death of a parent, whether beloved or despised, should free one finally into adulthood. But if that is so, then what am I doing here?

When it is dark I drag the boat as far as I can out onto the lake, wrap myself in a blanket and get in. Although there is no moon, the bed of the lake glows pale in the starlight. Oarless, my boat drifts in a sea of stars. This is where we should have burned my father's body, on this little boat cast adrift on this dry lake. Not in the sterility of the brick crematorium in Rockhampton. That ceremony had no meaning beyond the gathering of family and friends. Our rituals have become so eviscerated, so antiseptic, it is impossible to engage in them in any meaningful way. Or at least that is my experience. I wonder if I was to wound myself, like the Aborigines with their sorry business, would it release the bloody congealed accumulation of a lifetime's attachment?

My boat is sinking in stars, and Sam the dog has suddenly become frantic with fright, trembling and whining. Have I roused the local spirits? They might remember me. I used to dream here, skin brown as toffee, floating on the milky water, nothing in my head but the sensation of water and sun on skin. This place mapped itself into my body then, and breaks out on my adult self like stigmata.

Whether it is local spirits or my own demons I've raised, they have got the better of both of us. Sam's behaviour has completely unnerved me. I give up my vigil and leave my stranded craft for the safety of my swag and the fire. The dog digs in as close as he can get, and I pull the groundsheet over my head to shut out the reeling stars.

I WAKE TO A STEADY WIND blowing across the surface of the lake. It becomes stronger as the morning wears on. I try to paint a couple of gouaches but can make no sense of them. Conventional forms of representation seem to carry no meaning, and I don't know where to begin finding a means of recording this experience. I make pencil drawings of the ti-tree, the same trees under which my brother and I camped as children. The drawings are perfunctory. I cannot find the necessary detachment or focus to work properly, and have neither the skill nor the insight to translate the inscription these stunted trees make on the sand and against the skyline. The pencil stops moving across the sketchbook on my knees, and I am enclosed in one of those autistic moments when everything slips into isolated sharp focus, without sense or connection, absolute and unrecognisable. The shapes of light framed by branches, the shapes of shadows enclosed by sunlight, hold together in a vibrating stasis, a perfect balance between thing and non-thing beyond which there is nowhere to go.

I want to transcribe the marks and shapes which would represent a shared language of form and colour and light. I want to make visible the things this country makes me feel, and the things which have nothing to do with me and my personal quest. I feel the isolation in which so many artists work, attempting to dredge out of personal mythologies some form or image which will redeem the individual experience and make it part of something larger.

THE GROUNDSHEET HAS BECOME a kind of map, to record the day to day immediacy of the journey. The underside, which is serving as a swag cover and accumulating the ash and dust of each campsite, is becoming a travel-stained register of the trip in its own right. There did not seem to be an appropriate moment to bring it out at the women's ceremony, which would have provided all sorts of possibilities for marks and traces. Now I am sorry, and annoyed with myself. The groundsheet is raw material. I am sleeping in it, so that it must be absorbing the overflow of my dreams and confusion. Like a kind of Turin shroud, bearing the imprint of a transformative journey. What a pretentious notion. I could call it the Mongrel shroud.

This is supposed to be an artist's journey. But I am losing the boundaries between doing the work and paying homage to the pilgrimage it is turning into. My perception shifts constantly from surface to horizon to surface. Somewhere between the two is the narrative zone, the place where stories like the one I am tracing occur. It is a zone which seems transparent, fragile, provisional. It exists in the memory and the imagination as much as it exists in real space. There are the threads of journeys, thin lines connecting nodes from which activity radiates. It reflects the Aboriginal model, the line of sites connected by a track. It is a place which is about relationships, a psychological and a mythological zone. If you can't locate yourself in some sort of narrative or myth, you can't survive for too long in this country. It needs to be a strong story to take its place out here, and it needs to be something that comes from the country itself.

I am overtaken by the need to walk and touch, to feel earth and foliage against skin. It is as if there is an agreement between earth and flesh that draws them together. More and more as I try to make work that deals with the country, I feel the need for this physical encounter, something which cuts through the distance which drawing and painting force.

I walk barefoot, looking down, at tracks and the evidence of creatures, the hollows and nests and burrows they make, at the things which grow and the traces of the things which have died, at the colours and textures of stone and sand and soil. I remember the way it is when you live and work in the country. You are constantly looking at the tracks of cattle and horses or the tracks of vehicles, dingo tracks, kangaroo, emu, goanna, snake, pussycat, bandicoot. It is the way you know the country is busy, alive.

There are the tracks of a dingo, half erased in the soft sand. Near Flint Creek the feathers of a plains turkey are spread about among clumps of spinifex. The downy pale fluff of the underfeathers, evidence of killing, blur the sharp edges of a turpentine bush, as if it had burst suddenly into bloom.

I scoop out the sandy centre of a clump of spinifex. This is real spinifex, with its woody blue-grey base. The larger the circle of spiny foliage, the older the plant. I collect the largest of the scattered turkey feathers and line the scooped hole, feathering the nest within the harsh grey spikes of the spinifex. This act comes closer than any drawing I have done to reflecting a truth about this country. The wind nibbles the edges of the nest, and the feathers pulse gently. They will blow away soon enough, and sand will fill the hollow.

SAM SKULKS ABOUT LOOKING like a blue dingo while I pack up the camp. There used to be black dingoes around here, with tan feet and white-tipped tails. Sometimes at night one would cross my path when I was walking, or I would glimpse a black shape among the anthills in the late afternoon. The massive red forms of the anthills recede to the horizon, as if a crazed sculptor had lurched across the landscape attempting to create an archetypal form. When we built the airstrip we had to blast the anthills off with gelignite. My father brought home buckets full of monstrous white ants for the chooks to eat, and the flavour contaminated the eggs for days. My brothers and sister called one of the anthills near the lake Friend Anthill and used to perch on its summit, but I cannot remember which one it was.

Before leaving I make a few notes in my journal. The cold wind blows dust in my eyes, my nose runs and the ink blurs on the page.

My maps grow stranger. I do not contrive this. I do not even understand what the marks mean any more. The mud men watch me intently, and they come when I have finished and ponder over the marks and copy them. Sometimes they urinate on the symbols and plaster the resulting mud on their faces and genitals.

I move about blankly on the lake surface, inscribing, digging, scattering pigments, laying out arrangements of small stones. The maps become more intricate and precise, yet often I have no recollection of what I have done. Sometimes I fall and lie on the crusted salty clay for hours at a time. The child has taken to following me about, like a small gnome in her protective burnous. When I have a falling fit she waits for a time and then rouses me. The mud men creep out and watch me, but they do not help me. Their eyes peer out of cracked clay masks, spit collecting in the corners of their mouths and turning to muddy slime. No-one understands the purpose of the mud men any longer. It is believed that they were once shamans and holy men, but they have become something else now. It seems they are always somewhere about, at the periphery of vision, scratching themselves, defecating, fondling their genitals, occasionally breaking into furious biting scuffles. Their bodies are plastered with dried whitish clay, sometimes decorated with feathers and bits of grass, and they are always watching.

22

The drive from Lake Ruth to Wild Potato Bore takes me along the edge of the mulga, the road crossing the limestone spines which break at intervals through the surface of the country. This is where we used to find grinding stones, worn almost through, and the wild potatoes for which it is named. The stockmen showed us how to look for cracks radiating out from the base of the plant, evidence of the tuber growing a metre or so beneath the surface. I have watched an old woman tap with the sharp end of a crowbar, sensitive as radar, and read in the echo the size of the root, to judge whether it is worth digging for.

A fence line runs now from the bore to the west of the old stock camp, where a few lopsided posts mark the site of the bough shed. It was one of the main stock camps, a short run from the homestead. As children we all began our apprenticeship here, coming out for a few days at a time. It is easy country, open grass plains with pockets of gidgee and mulga.

THE GIRL IS FIFTEEN, WITH cropped dark hair and a thin bespectacled face. In the blue cotton shirt and jeans she could easily pass for a boy. The horse she rides is tall and black and elegant, with a broad white blaze and one long white sock. She sits him comfortably, relaxed in the heavy stock saddle, riding out on the wing of the small mob. From time to time she glances down at the silhouetted shadow she and the horse make, squares her shoulders and adjusts her hat to a more rakish angle. The spectacles don't show up in the shadow. Today she is relishing being in charge of a mob, with her brother and his friend as offsiders. The dreamy voluptuary of the lake is banished for the time being, replaced by this straight-backed, square-jawed stockman with eyes narrow and hooded from gazing into the limitless distance. This girl is familiar, but I need the device of the third person in order to see her properly. She inhabits her world uncritically, an intense adolescent world in which every moment and event is self-referential and self-contained. I see her with a kind of appalled insight, knowing what the almost quarter century which separates us holds for her.

Her brother rides on the other wing, a freckled boy with alert bright brown eyes, small for his eleven years. Already he shows the mark of a good horseman, a certain fluency of movement, a balance perfectly tuned to the gait of the grey horse. She likes him well enough, most of the time, though he has pulled free of his role as younger brother since she went away to school, and already his skill as a stockman equals her own. But today he doesn't care for the boredom of riding with this little quiet mob and calls to his friend at the tail that he has spotted fresh goanna tracks. Her brother's friend is older and bigger and quieter. A trace of Aboriginal blood shows in his smooth golden face and gives him a faintly Chinese look. The two boys ride out, away from the mob, to pursue the goanna, and she watches them go with irritation. She can manage well enough on her own but is angered that they treat her so cavalierly, that they are such boys, and irresponsible. If they lose the mob it will be her fault because she has been left in charge. The boys flush the goanna from a clump of grass and pursue it with shouts and yells. The long yellow lizard runs for its life, its reptile head up, eyes bolting, but the boys run it down. Her brother clubs it with a stick and throws it over the pommel of his saddle.

They bring the mob in to the bore and pull back to the shade of a bloodwood tree while the animals drink. They have been left for several days in charge of the weaners, which must be tailed out each day to feed and taken several miles to the bore to drink, before being yarded for the night in the small holding paddock. The children take it in turns to water their horses, then push the little mob together. The girl takes the lead and the two boys bring up the tail. To ride in the lead is a pleasure she rarely experiences, being usually relegated to the tail with the dust and stragglers. The weaners are docile and follow her readily along the cattle pads and into the holding paddock.

By sundown the riders are back at the camp, horses rubbed down and hobbled out, the goanna in the coals and the billy simmering. Cooked satisfactorily in its own charred skin, the goanna is broken in pieces and passed around with pieces of damper. For a treat the girl makes custard and stewed fruit for desert. She does not mind cooking on the campfire, in fact enjoys the challenge of cooking in these circumstances. This is a trait she carries into adult life, always happier to cook on an open fire with limited options than in a fully-equipped kitchen with everything to hand.

Her brother tells of his first time with the droving camp, before the family had moved out to the station. He thought the damper was a kind of magic pudding, constantly renewing itself, eaten at every meal but always there for the next. At last he discovered Long Johnny the cook mixing the dough of flour and water and baking powder, burying it in the camp oven and producing a fresh damper out of a hole in the ground. He made a damper himself then, a boy-sized one in a tobacco tin. There is an old black and white photograph taken of him at that time, a small figure in an oversized hat and boots, standing pensively beside a clump of spinifex, a rein draped over his arm and a horse's head poking into the picture on the upper right. The stance is self-consciously adult. It could be the prototype image for the Drover's Kid.

There is a rat plague moving across the country, followed closely by feral cats. Her brother is determined to catch enough rats to make a rat-skin coat, and sets traps around the camp. He forgets to mention this, until they start to go off like gunshots as the rats make their night-time move on the camp. The girl and the friend look at each other in alarm at the risks they have taken of losing a finger or toe. During the night a big rat comes snuffling onto the girl's swag. Her brother sees it and throws his boot, which hits the rat. It also hits the girl, so she wakes to the sight of a half-stunned rat stumbling off into the dark pursued by a small boy wearing nothing but a shirt. She threatens him with violence, and he tells her that the rat coat is for her.

I COULD NOT GET OUT OF my head the need to come back to this country. I have imagined this trip, many times. In the imagined journey there are no blank spaces. Every minute counts for something, every perception is recorded. It is evident from the amount of artist's materials I have brought with me that the journey was going to be intensely productive. I was going to draw, paint, record, rub, layer, trace. I was going to document every impression, every fragment that conjured memory and change, anything and everything that might have some relevance to my personal odyssey. There are oil sticks, gouache and watercolour, bitumen and pastels, tissue paper, drawing paper and canvas.

I have used almost nothing. I have managed to write up my journal, and I have managed to keep the groundsheet going. That is all. The rest of my energy is taken up with simply being here. It is a long time since I have felt anything with this level of intensity. A lot of the time I simply get in the car and drive, so as not to think. There are times when I have neither the will nor the desire to pay attention. I wish I had not given up smoking. Then I could sit still in various places and smoke and not think.

Now, here, every idea I have ever had seems irrelevant. The women's ceremony has shaken me out of the notion that I have any real knowledge of, or relationship with, Aborigines and their culture. The stories I have told to city friends, that have given my life a glamorous and exotic edge, seem like flimsy posturing. What is real is the discomfort, the blank space, the awkwardness, the recognition that one earns the right to a relationship through time spent with people and country, and that in recent years I have not spent that time. My relationship with the country belongs to the past. Instead of being shattered by this insight, I am relieved. It lets me off. I do not have to go on wearing the identity I have created for myself. I can decide whether or not to begin to spend the time, to build up a relationship based on the reality of this place as it is now, and the people who live here now. Or I can leave it behind.

FROM WILD POTATO I HEAD north to Andesite Plain. My father named it after the sandstone outcrops which characterise this part of the country, but I don't think the name is being used any more. I have ridden this way many times, setting out just after sunrise from the Wild Potato camp to muster the plains country and the mulga to the north. The horses liked this country, the sweet water from the bore and the open sweep of the grass plains. The stallion mobs ran here for preference, and when the mustering season was over the stock horses formed their small eunuch bands or joined up with the big mobs of mares and colts and foals.

There are no horses here today. I see from my map that the plains have been fenced in. A wild orange tree stands alone, bearing several large fruit. The black stockmen used to say the fruit was 'cooked' when it was ripe. I can't reach the fruit to tell whether it is cooked, even when I drive the Suzuki close to the tree and stand on the roof. My attempts to knock it down with a shovel are unsuccessful.

While my attempt to get some bush tucker is being frustrated a big red kangaroo hops slowly across my wheel tracks. He is the only roo I have seen this trip, a measure of the dry time. He echoes the single kangaroo of Davidson's journal, and again in my father's stock-route report.

> Just after leaving the solitary hill we sighted a red kangaroo. This was the first and only one we had seen.

> Here we saw our first animal life since Mt Doreen—a kangaroo.

Their kangaroos were a little further west, but it is clear that each journey must cross the path of a kangaroo. Somewhere I read that there is an ancestral track through this country which is the track of the two kangaroos. As I watch from my vantage point on the roof of the Suzuki the big roo makes steadily towards the fence line, which stretches along the ironstone ridge and away down through the softer sandy country towards the bore. There is an invisible point of intersection, where the dreaming track angles through from the north-east, making for the big salt-lake systems to the south-west.

The ancestral kangaroo is caught momentarily by the unexpected barbed wire of the fence line, which was not here when he last travelled. Blood spills from a torn thigh, and where it spots the ground small fierce bloody creatures burst forth and scurry away shrieking.

All over the country are these points of intersection, hot spots where the new maps overlay the old. This is our inheritance. Here the old maps are still visible. The people who know the old maps are building the fence lines now.

I drive on to Questionmark Bore. It is named for the shape of the mulga scrub which surrounds it. I am reluctant to camp at the bores, as I have been told dingo baits are put out every year. Sam is such a scavenger he is bound to pick up a bait, so I have to keep him tied up all the time. There is a set of cattle yards at Questionmark, which I examine with professional curiosity. From time to time I glimpse another destiny from the one I have chosen, in which I stayed out here. The prospect seduces and appals me. In the gap between this moment and the last time I stood in this place lie all the improbabilities and choices and contradictions that have brought me back to this place and this moment.

Briefly I stand shoulder to shoulder with the other one,

the one who stayed. We eye one another across the top rail of the yards. She looks much older than I do. Twenty years in this climate has a price. Lean and brown, turkey-necked, the perm looking a bit ragged under the Akubra, this other woman has a no-nonsense quality, sure of herself within the boundaries of this world. Sam gives her the once-over, and returns to my side of the fence. He can tell at a glance *she* wouldn't let him sleep in the cab of the Suzuki.

There is no evidence in her of the remnants of protracted adolescence which characterise so many of my generation. It is not just the result of time and weather. Her face has a certain cast I have often seen among people who spend their lives on the land. It is a peculiar and rather attractive mixture of philosophical acceptance of the vicissitudes of nature, governments and markets, and an unshakeable faith in the rightness of one's own point of view. She has not kept her options open. This is life. This is her life. She has made decisions and acted on them and worn the consequences. She knows the weight of responsibility for wrong decisions. She knows what it is to be helpless before acts of nature. The relentless conflagrations of immense spinifex fires, the country reduced again and again by drought. Wet seasons which cut roads for months and lay surface waters which tempt stock away into the desert beyond the point of no return. Market collapses and draconian government policies, the escalation of costs and erosion of income, the inevitable legacy of life on the land, this is all part of her knowledge. And something else. The country has worked on her, pared her down. She is comfortable here in a way that I am not.

She leans against a timber post in the narrow shadow it provides and pulls out a tobacco pouch, sticks the cigarette paper to her bottom lip while she extracts the tobacco. It is all done with a certain ritual deliberation, which allows for the place and the moment to be quietly acknowledged. When she fits the rolled cigarette into a short holder, the lurch of recognition shocks and amuses me. It is done for practical reasons, but there is no doubt it implies a certain sense of style. The familiar gesture of cupped palms, which was my father's, protects the lighted match, although for the moment there is no wind. I can taste the smoke of that first inhalation, sharp and aromatic. I can feel the way her body leans more deeply into its propped stance with the exhalation.

She looks across the expanse of the stockyards to the windmill, which does not turn. There is no hurry. The cigarette burns slowly. Along with the smoke she takes in the stillness of place and moment. After a time she treads the butt under a boot heel, walks over and climbs the side of the tank to check the water level. There is a mess of sodden floating feathers and stinking fragments in the tank. She fishes it out with the long wooden pole that has been left there for this purpose, pulls a face as she has to grab the unsavoury bundle. A brief circuit of tank and trough to check the float valve and to look at tracks. She is reading tracks and signs that I have forgotten. Signs of how many cattle are watering here and where they are feeding out, whether it will be necessary to move some to another bore, whether the dingo population is building up. The dust and the light, the dry grass and the wind that is not blowing carry for her refinements of information at which I can barely guess. Scraps of forgotten knowledge stir in some part of my mind and slide away again, fragments of a language I have lost.

There is something in the way she takes stock, pays attention, that is familiar. It suggests that she does not often make mistakes. This country is hard on mistakes, people die of them. And there is a moral dimension to it. Mistakes are the results of carelessness and stupidity and loss of nerve. From the time she was a girl she has had to prove that she is fit for the country. The set of her shoulders and the economy of her movements indicate she has proved that fitness. I suspect that she is inclined to judge the mistakes of others.

She squats in the shade of the stock tank, back propped against the galvanised metal, and produces a small sketchbook. This is evidently a familiar ritual, accompanied by the rolling of another cigarette, a flicking through pages to examine earlier sketches. They are predictable enough. Pencil drawings of carcasses and dead trees, some accomplished lively drawings of drafting and branding, colour notes and thumbnail roughs for paintings. There are hints of John Olsen and Fred Williams in the stretched spaces with their hieroglyphs of trees and anthills.

I take for granted she has not paid attention to the needs which took me away from this country. The choice of place, and the practical requirements of living here, have taken precedence over the journey away from place and towards the self. She does not submit her divided soul to the process of the work. She does not know about walking blind until the work reveals itself, and the humility it imposes, though she has occasional intimations of it. Her desire to paint is a desire to pay homage to this country and its people. She would like to do more, but there is never the time. She reminds me of my father. She scares the hell out of me. The merest shift and she is me.

The pages of the notebook flicker. I see that they are covered with words. The woman has become very still, as if watching some wild creature which has revealed itself. The handwriting is joltingly familiar.

The mapmaker walks out onto the surface of the dry lake. She carries with her the tools of her trade, the carved sticks and coloured sand with which to draw this day's map on the broken surface. In the night the wind has blown away all but a few traces of yesterday's work, and it still blows. Small powdery drifts of dust fly up from her feet as she walks. She kneels and begins to scoop out a long shallow shape, like a shield, or one of the long boats they used to sail before the lakes dried up.

The digging is a slow process, with only her hands and the digging stick as tools. When she has completed it to her satisfaction she carefully shapes the mound of displaced sand into the reverse form. From her satchel she takes a powdery block of ochre, deep red in colour, and rubs off a fine layer until both the mound and the hollow are coated with it. Even as she completes it the wind lifts the surface of the mound and begins to disperse it. As she walks away her retreating footprints fill with a fine smear of red-stained dust.

I stare at the words, and she stares directly at me. *Don't make assumptions about me,* her look says. *Stick to what you know.* She stubs out her cigarette, flips the notebook shut and gets to her feet. I watch her walk away from me into the dappled shade of the mulga, until the blue of her shirt and jeans is lost in the blue afternoon.

I AM SUDDENLY OVERWHELMED by a desire not to be here. This monotony of mulga scrub and red cattle-powdered earth confronts me with the raw stuff of my own irrelevance. A cappuccino in an Oxford Street coffee shop, a bit of window-shopping, a good escapist film. That is the way I would like to spend the afternoon. I make my coffee on the gas stove and eat a can of sardines straight from the tin. Somewhere among my gear is a Muriel Spark novel. It is a strange, disturbing little book, but too short. In a couple of hours I have finished it. I wish I had brought more escapist reading. One of those interminable Iris Murdoch novels full of people having ethical crises, or John Le Carre, with his world-weary spymasters and grey European borderlands. Anything to get away from here.

But I meant to pay attention, make every moment count. My travelling books include Lucy Lippard's *Overlay*, and Deleuze and Guattari's *Nomadology*, which I have never been able to read. I brought it with me on the principle that with absolutely nothing else to read I would be forced to persevere. The convoluted language makes a kind of mad sense in this setting, among the dusty mulga trees. I march around the cattle yards declaiming passages aloud.

—The critique of the hylomorphic schema is based on 'the existence, between form and matter, of a zone of medium and intermediary dimension', of energetic, molecular dimension—a space unto itself (*un espace propre*) that deploys its materiality through matter . . .

I articulate the parentheses and the inverted commas for the benefit of the listening crows, which cark derisively whenever I stop for breath. I climb onto the top rail and fling sentences at them.

—The primary determination of the nomad is that he occupies and holds a smooth space . . .

The crows are not impressed, in spite of the parentheses. I turn a few pages and try again.

—The sedentary assemblages and State apparatuses effect a capture of the phylum, put the traits of expression into a form or a code, make the holes resonate together ...

It is no good. By this time the crows are hysterical, and so am I.

I DECIDE TO CONTINUE THE bore run and camp at Kim's Bore, my namesake. They have misspelled it as Kym's Bore. So much for posterity. Again there is a fence line, a gate. I take Sam for a walk, on a lead so there is no chance of him picking up a bait. The country is red and dry, dry. The sunset blazes crimson and gold through the blades of the windmill, an iconic Outback image. Topnotch pigeons burst past me in a soft grey flurry. I want to fling myself into a wild, bursting embrace of all this. Instead I wash my hair, rinse a few clothes and cook a rice pudding in the camp oven.

It is the time between day and night that is profound with melancholy. My attempt to stave it off with domestic chores fails. I sit by my campfire and accept it, knowing it will pass. There is a passage in that strange and wonderful book *The Soul of the Ape*, in which the South African scientist Eugene Marais describes the behaviour of the baboon troupe he studied. At sunset the busy activities of the day are suddenly curtailed, and silence falls among the baboons. Babies seek the comfort of their mothers, and adolescents gather to gaze towards the fading western horizon. Among the adult animals a kind of grief takes hold, and as darkness falls they call out in deep sorrow at the day's ending. To Marais this was evidence of an inherent pain of consciousness, shared with humans and articulated in the moment when day shifts into night.

I watch the leaping flames and pay attention to these deep stirrings of primate grief. My sophisticated identity crisis flares briefly and goes out in the swooping darkness, and for a moment I am outside myself, feeling truly the pain of consciousness and the day's death.

In my swag, sleep refuses to come. The Cross turns slowly above me, the Milky Way streams across the night sky, and my mind turns and streams with it. I am tormented and disturbed by what I find out here. It seems I cannot leave it alone. I know that this place and these people are intensely important. Once I would have claimed knowledge and empathy with it and them. Now I stand outside it all, transfixed and silenced. The picture I had of my life is crazing over like a shattered mirror, every fragment containing a distorted reflection.

Somewhere in all of this is the story I am trying not to tell. Along a route marked by campsites, bores, claypans and sand ridges I am tracing the thread of a life which is in large part my own life, a personality whose traits not only deeply influenced me but are my own traits, a temperament which is mirrored by my own. I came here to lay the ghost of my father, and am confronted instead with myself.

It was from my father that I got the notion of the sublime in landscape, and of the land as a site of redemption. But as I pursue his memory out here, he recedes from me and from this place, and I am left with a shadow, an after-image. I cannot see him for the shadow cast by my own presence.

My father's life had in it certain focal acts. One of them was the stock-route trip. Another was the early years of establishing Mongrel Downs, then the remotest cattle station in Australia. The events are the stuff from which legend is formed, and they were shaped into a story which has embedded itself into the fabric of my family's and my own history, until it seems that all other events gain significance only in relation to these legendary acts.

Am I attempting to do the same thing with my own journey? To create a focal act which will displace those of my father. It seems likely. This journey is like a cable which attaches my past to my future. Slowly, deliberately, with all the skills I have, I am attempting to weave another story. It contains my father's myth, but it has another layer that is my own, which parallels my father's but is profoundly different in its infrastructure. Is this how I attempt to free myself, by acknowledging the parallels, and within those similarities make a story that is very different in its intention?

Or is what I am doing a kind of heresy, an unmaking? For want of a better word I call it art, which my father would have seen as self-indulgent posturing. (And there are moments when I see it the same way.) It is as if I have dragged all my own messy baggage onto his territory and thrown it down like a challenge.

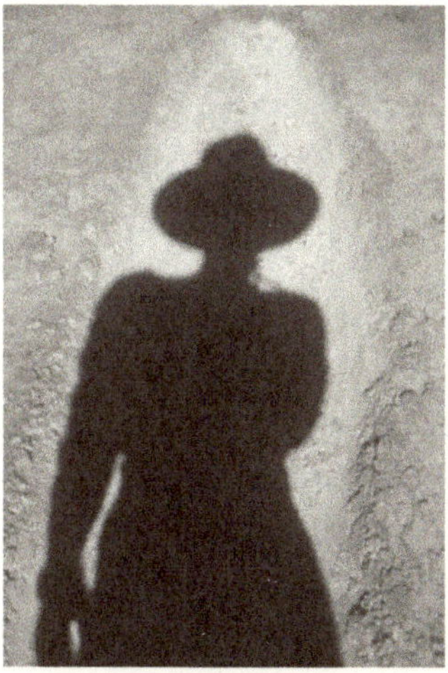

23

ALTHOUGH THERE WERE TIMES when my father retreated behind the persona of the laconic bushman or into a punishing silence, in fact he liked to talk. We are a family of talkers, but my father held the floor when he chose. When my father talked I listened.

I knew when to throw in the right cues. I wanted to hear his stories. I was younger then, and I believed everything. I made myself in his image. Later, when I tried to get free of it, I didn't know how to begin. I had never developed the habit of rebellion, only the habit of concealment. Did he feel that slow withdrawal of perfect faith, in spite of my attempts to hide it? I was angry when I finally started seeing his feet of clay, and how they held me down too.

He held my life in thrall for all of my childhood and much of my adult life. It was not intentional. Somewhere in the emotional space between a man and his first child, who was a much-loved daughter, an edifice was created that was both real and imaginary. It existed in the minds of the father and daughter as a marvellous bond of almost perfect understanding. And so it was, so long as the daughter was a child. I have watched friends and brothers who have become the fathers of daughters, and it is a miracle of tenderness. It is the most delicate, fraught and poignant of bonds.

⁓

MY FATHER WAS DARK-HAIRED and good looking as a young man. He kept his hair, which as he aged became a silvery mane. He disliked haircuts, and his hair was usually curling on his collar, at which point he had been known to saw the ends off with a pocket knife. He had a fine sense of the absurd. When relaxed and on his own ground he was excellent company, though usually as the centre of attention. I used to feel uncomfortable if others took the limelight away from him for too long. He read with penetrating and perceptive intelligence, but was immensely scathing of the theoretical that was not mediated by practical experience. He needed to be right about things. It was impossible to argue with him, it became a personal affront. We didn't argue. It was easier not to.

He taught me how to do things. I learned to drive when I could barely see over the bonnet of the Landcruiser. He bought me a pony and taught me the rudiments of riding. He taught me how to weld, how to use tools, how to make things and fix things. He taught me how to think my way into things, work them out, not be intimidated. And how to question and challenge authority, as long as it wasn't his.

From him I learned the importance of nature, the value of small daily things, how to be trusting and trustworthy, to be respectful of human beings who deserved respect. All of us learned by example to value the Aboriginal world that surrounded us, and to learn from it. From time to time I heard my father referred to as 'a bit of a blackfellow-lover'. In the

Territory of that time this was considered unusual and rather eccentric. In my father's case it was applied because he had a reputation for fairness which he extended regardless of colour. When he was a young superintendent on Hooker Creek, he took some of the Aborigines with him on a trip to Katherine. One of the boys came to him and said the shopkeeper had cheated him, and my father went with him back to the store and confronted the shopkeeper. It turned out he'd short-changed the boy a penny—A penny's a penny, and anyway it's the principle that matters, insisted my father, feeling a complete fool. It's one of the things that never changed. Even at sixty that twenty-five year old was still there, prepared to make a fool of himself defending a boy's right to his penny.

⁓

MY FATHER WAS SUSPICIOUS of anything that smacked of psychology, and deeply uncomfortable with any public expression of emotion. He described it as *spilling your guts* or, ironically, *expressing your innermost feelings*. I have some sympathy with his attitude, especially after the excesses that have resulted from a generation in search of its inner child.

But he was extreme, probably because he had a kind of terror of exposing himself. He was like someone who had experienced a religious upbringing, and had failed its principles in some profound way. I don't know what it was he was afraid of exposing.

It may have a fairly simple explanation. My father was a shy, self-conscious boy who felt deeply the inadequacies of his education and social background. Drink set him free, allowed him to experience himself as clever, charming, talented—all things he was by nature. But the monster lurked in a genetic predisposition to alcoholism, a severe form which attacks the brain and causes profound personality change, eventually irreversible. There are hints, though no hard evidence, that this disease may have been the reason for his father's abandonment to the orphanage. It wouldn't be the first time the black dog of alcoholism has haunted an Irish family down the generations.

So there was my father. Handsome, funny, charming, intelligent, honest, extremely competent at everything he took on, a good horseman, any child's hero. And there was my other father. Unpredictable, volatile, sentimental, morose, sensitive to every imagined slight or challenge. I loved them both, the one with uncomplicated delight, the other with great caution, which slipped at times into vertigo and panic.

The Outback was a serious drinking culture, kept in check more by geography than by design. The spree after a stint out bush was standard practice, and the awesome excesses some drinkers achieved were part of the Territory folklore. By the time my father's drinking became visible as a problem, he was in bad trouble, having had several seizures during which he blacked out, each one causing cumulative brain damage. The dark personality was present like a stain even when he was in his lighter, cheerful mode.

When he understood finally that his drinking was a disease that was killing him and damaging his family, he stopped. But the shadow never left him. Maybe it had always been there. My mother says not, but she has a selective memory. I don't think he ever forgave himself for his weakness, and the social ease that alcohol had given him was gone for good.

Although my father stopped drinking when I was in my early teens, the relationship between us had been formed in the drinking years. The shadow personality spoke directly to something in my own nature, an awareness of the damage people could do to each other, of the paradoxical nature of love. One could neither choose love nor evade it. It was a force of nature, a direct link to the soul. It gave meaning and abolished it. Nothing could be done about love, particularly a child's love, which has no measures or boundaries.

I have my little suitcase of baggage, left over from that time. I have unpacked it often over the years, taken out the contents and examined them, thrown out anything that has become threadbare and moth-eaten. I have found strange cherished half-forgotten things, which I have carefully folded and put back, and unlabelled parcels pushed away at the bottom which I have not dared to unwrap. It is a Pandora's box. I never know when I open it what may suddenly fly out into the world, leaving me shaken and amazed.

The suitcase weighs differently at different times. There was a time when it seemed unable to contain the awkward shape of my confusion and fear. Mostly these days it travels fairly lightly, though at the moment it has the additional weight of maps and diaries, and a tea tin containing a scraping of clay and ashes.

I have felt craven before various social frameworks, eager to please, to not be found out. It has seemed as if all around me are forms and structures which have an a priori existence, within which authority is vested by some ordained right. The things I have wanted for my life have not been compatible with these structures. It has been necessary to find gaps and holes through which to move, as unobtrusively as possible. A strange and precious byproduct has been the discovery in these gaps of the raw materials of art. I have tried to avoid being unmasked and forced to make a stand, not sure whether I have the necessary courage to do it. Many of the choices I made were influenced and encouraged by my father. His authority stood stronger than the broader social authority. As long as he approved the direction I chose for my life, I could withstand the pressures and expectations from other quarters. Somewhere in the suitcase is a package labelled 'Authority', and this trip has something to do with it. It is about telling this man in my head, this 'father', who has taken up the space the dead man left, that I no longer need him to authenticate me.

AT BOARDING SCHOOL, IN THE neat box pleats of her tartan uniform and the circumscribed symmetry of her days, the place the girl called home seemed as improbable to her as it did to her schoolmates and teachers. She began to wonder whether she had simply made it up. Sometimes she did make it up. She discovered that people were inclined to disbelieve the true things she told them and to believe the more outlandish inventions. She invented her home as a counterpoint to the unrelenting femaleness of the school. At the same time she became absorbed in the finely-tuned nuances of style and behaviour necessary to survive school life.

It demanded on all sides a kind of conformity, which was the conformity of tradition and social convention, the particular conformity on which the school's reputation was built, of producing young women of sound education and social conscience, who would be fine citizens and mothers and would help shore up the foundations of civilised behaviour. She was once given a thousand lines to write as a punishment, which gave her the opportunity to examine their meaning and repudiate them at length.

Obedience is essential if a civilised community is to be maintained.

She was not old enough, or knowledgeable enough, to cite historic examples of the dangers of obedience, but could only resist the premise as if her life depended on it. But this sort of conformity was visible and could be resisted.

It was the soft, small, constant barbs of girls she could not fight, that said, you are not one of us, you don't belong, your clothes are wrong, your words are wrong, you are wrong. They clustered like anemones and measured out with waving barbed tendrils their precise collective judgement, which applied to that place and that moment, which had nothing to do with family or society or the visible structures of school life, but was to do with a self-invented girl realm. Among them she was constantly alert, a chameleon child, ready to adjust her dress, her speech, her behaviour, if only she could grasp what it was that must be adjusted. She watched their mouths and their eyes. She was like a deaf child learning to lip-read.

On Sundays, walking to church in her white dress and gloves and panama hat, indistinguishable among fifty white-clad girls, the elegant suburban mansions giving off an odour of gentility, she could not believe that any other world was possible.

He stepped straight from the exotic realm of the Outback into the circumscribed boarding school world, and in that moment he authenticated her and the world she came from. He didn't look like the other girls' fathers, the wheat and sheep farmers who seemed diminished by their town clothes, who wore flat-brimmed hats and tweed jackets and waited in the car while their wives negotiated the release of daughters.

He had the bowed legs and gait of a horseman, the sides worn down on the heels of his high-heeled boots. The brim of his Akubra tilted down over his eyes, and his hair was black and curled about the collar of his blue shirt. He was deeply tanned and his eyes were hooded already from staring into the sun, though he was not yet forty. There was a hint of lawlessness about him. He walked into that inner sanctum of femaleness and prohibitions in his high-heeled boots and his rakish hat and plucked her from it.

Her friends watched her pack a few clothes, enough for several days. She did not know how long she would be away, or where she was going.

—That's really your father!

He looked the way he had always looked, but she saw him now with the eyes of the other girls.

That first night they stayed at the Adelphi Hotel, which was the flashest place she had ever stayed in, and ate in the grand dining room. The silver service waiter patronised them, which she noticed but her father didn't. Her school was teaching her to recognise refinements of class and manners. She loved the way her father was so direct and friendly, so that before long the waiter came out from behind his waiter's face and was friendly too. It turned out that he was a country boy from Narrikup who wanted to be a writer, and her father said—Good for you, if you're prepared to do a job like this, then you're bound to get wherever you want.

Her father had a mailbag with a change of clothes, and a damaged knee from a fall from a horse. He had escaped from hospital in Alice Springs and caught a plane to Perth in order to see her. No-one back home knew where he was. They plunged down the West Australian coast in a hired car, to some fictitious rendezvous in Albany. They were a pair of escapees, outlaws on the run. It was exhilarating and a little frightening. He stopped at the pub in every small coastal town to top up his dangerous spirit, and she sat in the car and waited for him unquestioningly. The pubs all looked the same, down at heel, with a midweek emptiness that gave them a clandestine air. She rolled cigarettes for him while he drove, sticking the paper to her bottom lip and breaking up the fine-cut tobacco with the heel of her hand. He said she was a good little mate.

The weather was dank and overcast. Albany was grey and cold, with an icy wind blowing sheets of fine rain. They stayed in a motel with grey walls and brown furniture. He said he needed to see someone, and went away for a time, then came back and took her to the drive-in in the gusting rain. Her eyes hurt from the cigarette smoke. Over the next couple of days they drove about aimlessly. The harbour was the colour of old tin, a lustreless pocket of trapped ocean, and the ships looked like stranded beasts.

She was not afraid while she was with him, only astounded into a knowledge that the forms of reality were so easily dislodged. This aimless flight through rain and fog with a strange man who was her father had become her reality. She knew he was in a tormented frame of mind, but she knew also that she would come to no harm while she was with him. She was his accomplice. In a curious way she felt protective towards him. So long as they stayed together no harm would come to either of them.

He drank steadily, leaving her at intervals, though never for long, to spend an hour in a strange bar. She wondered if he spoke to anyone on these occasions, but did not ask. Neither did she ask him if and when he intended to return her to school. His removal of her had been a rescue of a kind. At some point he seemed to come to a decision. He turned north then and took her back. She would just as soon have stayed with him, on the run. He charmed the matron for his anarchic removal of her, and was gone as suddenly as he had arrived.

She did not tell her schoolmates anything about where she had been. His visit had changed her status irrevocably. She did not feel bound to explain anything. She had been somewhere with him, another place, where the rules didn't apply. She knew now that such places existed, and that they were part of the real world.

I LOOK AT THE MYTHOLOGIAL options for daughters and they do not seem to be good. Iphigenia is sacrificed by Agamemnon to ensure a fair wind for Troy. Antigone's fate was to lead blind Oedipus about the stony hills of Greece until his death, and later to be walled up alive by her uncle for sprinkling earth on the unburied body of her brother. The miller's daughter paid with the loss of her hands for her father's deal with the devil.

But a closer reading shows something curious and interesting. Again and again daughters are cast out or incarcerated. They wander alone in the forest, or find themselves trapped in the presence of monsters and murderers. They do solitary penance away from the protective authority of the father, and they free themselves by this penance, this endurance. At this point they cease to be daughters and become women.

WHEN I FIRST READ *TRACKS*, Robyn Davidson's account of her camel trek across the desert to the West Australian coast, my response to it was ambivalent. I found the whole thing too close for comfort. She articulated too clearly the complicated impulses and female messiness and fears I hated in myself. There she was, raw and visible, a woman struggling as much with her own nature as with the practical and cultural obstacles involved in such a venture.

My father's reaction to the book was curious. He was oddly taken with her unflattering portrait of Alice Springs and its inhabitants, hugely impressed by her achievement, and found her introspection distasteful. He would hate this introspective tale of mine.

WITHOUT MY FATHER I SHOULD never have known this country. It was men who explored it, men who were driven to find gold and land, and by less tangible desires to penetrate into the unknown. It is fashionable these days to interpret these desires in sexual terms. I think this is a simplistic view, clever and cynical, which overlooks the imaginative, the spiritual and the pragmatic elements which were also a part of the impulse. When I was a child it was my father who authorised the way we moved about the country, who decreed where the tracks should go, who traced the boundaries and fence lines on mud maps. Now it seems equally clear that the country exercised its own authority, which was acknowledged to a greater or lesser degree by the men who developed it. It was as if another country lay concealed under the tracery of tracks, bores and fence lines. This was the country which took hold of my father.

Out here, travelling through my father's country, I understand that the 'father' in my head has grown hugely beyond the dimensions of the man I remember. The man I glimpse in the pages of the station diary is preoccupied with the responsibilities of the job he has taken on, the people who are dependent on him. There are moments when he loses sight of his wife and children and struggles to find his way back to them. Even from this distance I am too close to him to see him clearly. He carries about him a certain intensity, he is isolated without being self-contained. He expects a great deal of himself, and his family is an extension of himself.

When my father gave up drinking he also gave up much of his social persona, but he did not give up the reasons which had made him drink—the lack of confidence, the sense of having to prove himself, the fear of being found out. The irony of course is that there was nothing to find out. We already knew the boundaries and dimensions of his weaknesses. His integrity and his achievements easily balanced the ledger. But he was not a man to believe in the possibility of being loved regardless of flaws. Indeed he struggled with his own love for his flawed family, punishing us for our lapses in good sense and good judgement.

Things changed after we moved to Queensland. It was so much tougher than we'd anticipated. The collapse of the beef market made cattle worthless. My mother supported the family by taking a teaching job at one of the nearby mining towns. An unsympathetic federal government reinforced the growing siege mentality that was overtaking the bush. As soon as the market recovered, the country suffered a series of droughts. The family bonds tightened in those early years and we all worked on the station at every opportunity.

But there is a price for the bonds formed in hard times, especially on the land. Individual needs are subsumed in the larger difficulties, and we were not a family which encouraged emotional expression. My father's natural reclusiveness was reinforced by the country itself. The tall eucalypt forest and impenetrable brigalow scrub was enclosed and secretive. It was a kind of hideout, a wilderness big enough to allow him to maintain his dream, his own idea of who he was. Although he appreciated our help, he could not tolerate the intrusion of our expanding worlds into his territory. And he did not want to hold us back from developing independent lives. He wanted us to be gone, so we went. We all came home from time to time, slipping off parts of our identities at the front gate and driving into the world he'd created. It was like driving into his mind. Bits of it were stalled, and bits of it were fantastically rich. There wasn't really room for us in it, and yet we were enormously important to him. He loved to see us, but preferably one at a time, and not for too long.

My mother continued to teach, even when it was no longer necessary. Reclusiveness did not suit her, and she had become attached to her independence. She maintained her own working life and circle of friends, and came home on weekends and holidays. It was an arrangement which suited them both. My father's refusal to participate in social occasions was something we all took for granted. We did not expect him to make a speech as father of the groom when my brother Bob was married. We were not entirely sure that he would come to the wedding. He floored us all with a speech that was articulate and unselfconscious, a perfect balance of humour and warmth, utterly genuine. At Jim's wedding he did it again. They were the only public occasions at which I heard my father speak.

In an odd way these years were the most difficult for me with regard to my father. I was getting on with my own life, and the adjustment when I came to the station to visit was more and more difficult to make. He was always so delighted to see me. I think there were times when he was very lonely in his self-created isolation, and I still felt the sense of responsiblity towards him that had been established when I was a child. The work of running the station was far too much for one person, and his health was not particularly good. His authority was less assured, the vulnerability more visible. On every visit I felt the old pull to come back, to help out, to try to make everything all right, at the same time knowing it was absurd, that I would not be able to stand it, that in any case it was not what was required of me. What he needed was an empathetic listener, someone with whom he could discuss the ideas and thoughts that filled his mind while he mended fences and cut posts and laid pipelines. He needed someone to reassure him that the way he saw the world was legitimate, that the choices he had made for his life were good choices. I think too he wanted to know that I was happy.

Often when I drove away from these visits I would find myself in tears, and at the same time profoundly relieved to be gone. The relief caused me more pain than the sadness.

The thing I remember most about my father is his love of the land, his deep sense of identification with it, the sheer pleasure he took in it. This was something he carried with him from boyhood and which never changed. The boy was somehow always present in the delight he took in small details and events, the activities of birds and animals, the revelations of nature. He was not a cattleman at heart. When he looked at the country he did not see rolling acres and fat cattle. When he was younger he saw horizons, mystery, the unrevealed possibilities of the desert. Later he came to love the tall eucalypt forest and saw it as a respite, the place in which his spirit could be at home. It always seemed to him miraculous that he had somehow acquired such a tract of land. He was sceptical of the notion of ownership. He saw his relationship to land in terms of custodianship, an attitude he passed on to his children.

—It's always been here, he said. —It's your job to look after it for your lifetime, and then you pass on the responsibility to someone else.

I think this was a position which came naturally to him

and did not derive from Aboriginal attitudes towards their country.

The last time I saw my father there was a quiet affection between us. I had always known the dangerous ground, and it no longer cost me much to avoid it. There were still moments when he could provide for me a sense of comfort and security, of gentleness and generosity. I knew the art I was making would not meet with his approval, but we skirted around the contentious areas. He talked more and more about the importance of living close to nature, his gratitude for his life and family, the notion that life was full of checks and balances. He had evolved this philosophy through the hard years. It seemed to him that while things were difficult in terms of pratical survival, the family would be protected from misfortune and harm. As if there was a quota on luck, good and bad.

I have this memory of my father. We are sitting on the front verandah of the homestead. It is evening, and a few shafts of sunset are caught in the bougainvillea which spills its dark red flowers among the branches of a quinine tree. At his feet lies a cluster of animals, a small ancient fluffy white terrier, a geriatric black and white cat and a sleek and elegant grey cat, sole survivor of a feral litter. He is particularly fond of this wild cat, who emerged from the bush as a tiny kitten and climbed onto his boot. She follows him about now like a dog. The evening sounds of the bush are close, the hootings and croakings and scurryings taking over from the daylight voice of the country.

My father says—You have to forgive yourself, you have to give yourself some leeway for your life.

He says—If I had my time over again, I would choose to be an artist.

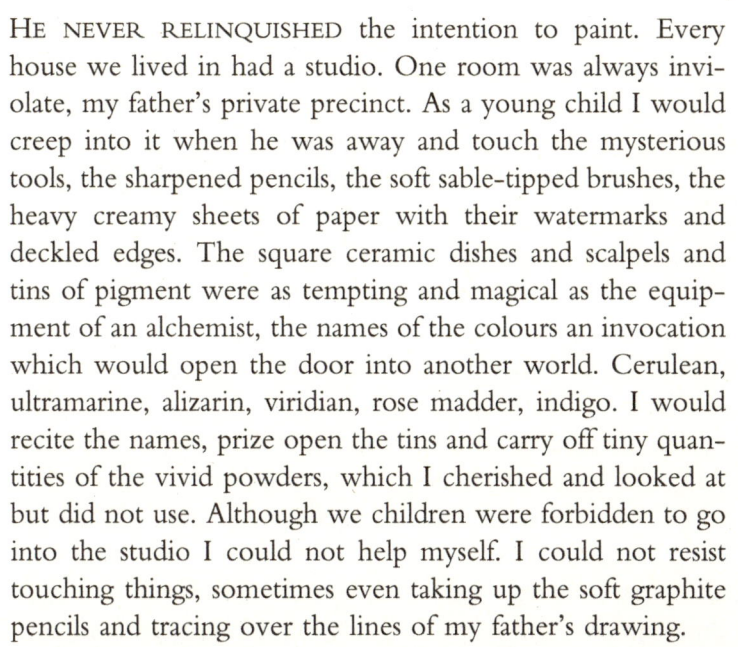

HE NEVER RELINQUISHED the intention to paint. Every house we lived in had a studio. One room was always inviolate, my father's private precinct. As a young child I would creep into it when he was away and touch the mysterious tools, the sharpened pencils, the soft sable-tipped brushes, the heavy creamy sheets of paper with their watermarks and deckled edges. The square ceramic dishes and scalpels and tins of pigment were as tempting and magical as the equipment of an alchemist, the names of the colours an invocation which would open the door into another world. Cerulean, ultramarine, alizarin, viridian, rose madder, indigo. I would recite the names, prize open the tins and carry off tiny quantities of the vivid powders, which I cherished and looked at but did not use. Although we children were forbidden to go into the studio I could not help myself. I could not resist touching things, sometimes even taking up the soft graphite pencils and tracing over the lines of my father's drawing.

He always seemed to know when I had been in the studio. I suspected the wooden artist's mannikin of telling tales. It crouched above the desk like a voodoo doll, knowing and malevolent, with its faceless head and fingerless hands. I inherited it, as I inherited the tins of partly used powders which I still hoard and still do not use. I do not like the mannikin, and I have never used it as a drawing prop. But I am superstitious about it, as if it has been witness to my first clandestine marks, which I attempted to conceal within my father's lines, and is witness now to the slow process through which I have come to make my own marks.

My father was angry when I inadvertently defaced his work, but he praised and encouraged my drawing and bought me my first set of oil paints. Art was our shared passion. Over the years we exchanged gifts of books and materials, and my tastes and influences bore the mark of my father's tastes and influences. He had a good eye and a respect for sound craftsmanship. He appreciated some forms of abstraction but was immensely scathing of the more esoteric aspects of modernism. Even now I cannot trust my initial response to a work of art and must examine whether my reaction stems from some learned prejudice. My first visit to the Van Gogh Museum in Amsterdam, at the age of twenty-five, was a revelation. My father was not much impressed with Van Gogh. I stood before the shimmering canvases and my head reeled. Paint rippled and exploded from surfaces, colour roared in my ears. My world turned upside down. I stood dazed before canvas after canvas, thinking, *This work is wonderful.* Thinking, *My father is wrong.* Thinking, *I can't tell him.*

He continued to draw and paint whenever he had the time, which was not often. The voice which is missing from the diary is everywhere present in the sketchbooks he filled and kept over the years. The drawings are strong and accomplished, whether brief sketches or more finished observations. There are the drawings he made to entertain himself and us. The drooling dragonlike creature made of sections of drainpipe, which lived on the other side of the plughole in the bathtub and which we called the drainosaur. And a wonderful series of giant anthills which were transformed into monstrous gorillas, dragging their knuckles and glowering from under beetling brows.

But the drawings are mostly of landscapes, the landscapes of memory and imagination as well as the landscape of his immediate surroundings. The notebooks are filled with the sketches he planned someday to turn into paintings. There are recurring motifs, the dance of cowled ghostly silhouettes of young desert oaks along a sand ridge, a solitary figure at the end of a line of fence posts, isolated by perspective and space. The voice, the sensibility is at once conventional and unique. It is a voice set firmly within the conventions of the pictorial narrative, but the story it has to tell is unique. It is impossible to guess what he might have done had he chosen art over country. There was no indication that he understood the choice would have been the deeper excursion into unknown country, but this is something I can never be sure of.

24

TIME SLOWS, OUT HERE. The life I drove away from only a few weeks ago has ceased to signify in any meaningful way. I cannot imagine returning to it. The morning rises over the mulga trees. My work has always been a step or two ahead of me. Often I don't understand it until long after it is done. The red bone shapes of my own printed flesh lie spread-eagled on the canvas groundsheet beneath me, a repetition of crosses which refuse to submit to the boundaries I have drawn for them. This body I inhabit, pale-skinned, female, unobtrusive, has announced itself emphatically, used its angry, ochre-coated physical presence to blot out the abstraction of the grid lines. Anarchic, sexual, it refuses to be reduced to an idea. *I am here*, it says. *I am real.*

I remember this body at seventeen, standing here, in this namesake place, on a cold winter night, feeling its own vigour and power. On the other side of the fire a man stood, a young man I knew well. If sexual tension could be rendered visible, it existed in the rippling edge of flame where it met the chill edge of cold air. This body, such a simple thing, could render inarticulate the man across the boundary of firelight, could cause him to suffer violently. It pleased me then, and even now causes me to smile. She was so young, and testing the edges of things she barely understood. She knew that the man was decent and would not force himself on her, in spite of their being alone in the firelit darkness, with no-one likely to come upon them for hours yet. She knew she would not cross the boundary, had not yet crossed it, that this was not the time and place. But she took a deep, childish pleasure (childish because she gave no thought to the man) in knowing he desired her and would not harm her. I pay her homage now, that self-contained girl who did not care that a man suffered, who knew she would wait until she was ready and make an offering of herself on her own terms. Who revelled in the cold space around her and the heat of the fire and her own heartless vivid self-fulness. It is she who has come forward after all these years of blurred edges, of feeling the needs of other people, of losing her charmed edge, and said—I am here. Remember me.

How long after this was it that she crossed that sexual boundary and encountered at first-hand the vulnerability of men, as well as her own? I welcome back the sharp-edged girl whose body has not been softened with experience and empathy. She has a kind of clear courage I have given away. She is a primitive. I don't regret that I have become civilised, but I need her fierce emphatic selfishness.

Sam is complaining that it is time I did something about him. If I am not going to let him off his lead, then I can at least take him for a walk. Reluctantly I get out of the swag, preoccupied, my mind swerving towards making the work, this process which for me has become the means through which I explore and engage with life. The body, using the body, the physical presence within the work, the defiant statement among the network of structures which so easily take control. A way of beating the intellectual tangle in which I inevitably become enmeshed. A way of holding together the thinking process and the unthinking process in a kind of poised tension.

I walk with my geriatric blue dog along the fence line, dragging him away from the old dried bones he finds irresistible, explaining that it is for his own good. He grins his comical toothless grin and tells me in his dog-language of musical wails that it is a dog's responsibility to investigate bones. For breakfast I make us both a treat, a stock-camp breakfast of johnny cakes made from damper mix, fried on the hotplate and drenched in golden syrup. Tonight I had better use some of the dried vegetables in the tuckerbox, or I will come down with scurvy. A flock of galahs take turns to sip at the water trickling from the overflow pipe on the stock tank, shuffling in an orderly queue along the pipe, erupting periodically into furious quarrels when one attempts to jump the queue.

Such luck, such a privilege to be here like this.

TO THE NORTH-WEST I CUT my earlier tracks at the Macfarlane's turnoff. A little further on is a tripod and pump-jack, which on my new map is marked as Century Bore. There is no storage tank, just a pipeline running to tanks which provide watering points through the extensive perennial grass plains to the south. These form the heart of the good pastoral country on which the Tanami Downs lease is based. Some time in the eighties the lease was bought by the Aboriginal Central Land Council, and it continues to run as a cattle station, usually under white management. When a new goldmine was developed on the eastern edge of the lease, along the ancient Warlpiri dreaming track which runs between Tanami and Inningarra, an agreement was struck with the traditional owners, who were entitled to royalties. Margaret Napurrula, Patricia's mother, had the stories of the country from her father and grandfather, though she was born in the Gordon Downs country to the north. This story is becoming more and more common since the dispersals and displacement of people from their traditional country. Once the place of conception conferred the birthright, but now it is more and more the handing down of stories and knowledge of traditional homelands. Margaret came back, with her adult children and extended family, and they live now in a small outstation a few kilometres from the homestead, threatened intermittently by land claims from other Warlpiri groups.

It seems that the last of the traditional people for this country moved away in the fifties and found their way north to Hooker Creek, south-east to Yuendumu and west to Balgo. This would always have been tough country to live in, entirely without permanent water before the stock-route bores were sunk, and a run of dry seasons would have curtailed movement through much of the country. Davidson's 1900 account makes reference to sighting smokes to the south-west of Mt Tracey, which would have put them on the edge of the Great Sandy Desert, and records the next sighting near the Smoke Hills to the north of here. By the time my family came here there were traces and remnants, but the people had gone. The stockmen who worked for us came from the north-west and went back to their own country for ceremonial business.

I am glad that the people have come back, and appreciative of the many ironies that are encapsulated in this isolated pocket of the country. Gold and cattle have made it possible for them to return, and now they are the employers of white managers to handle the white man's business of running cattle, and are recipients by virtue of traditional right to the spin-off of the white man's hunger for gold. I move about the country with their permission, readily given, since I too have come back for the country, with my own stories.

I drive south through the great yellow sweep of the plains, the day's direction dictated by a set of wheel tracks that will bring me to another site, another set of memories. A by-product of travelling alone is the steady erosion of reference points, of identity and personality. There is no-one on whom to exercise a personality but Sam the dog, and as long as I provide him with regular meals and a little yellow truck to ride in he does not care whether I am clever and witty, charming, morose or downright mean. The tracks I follow provide a structure for my days. The landmarks and intervals of the country I am crossing dictate the shapes of my emotions and my thoughts. To understand how much a sense of identity depends on being reflected in the eyes of others is a sobering experience. I have prided myself on having a clear mind, but the space out here has invaded it, breached the skull so that the thing I call self has got loose and is wandering about on the brittle plain, stalked by something primitive and wild (something that was always out there, or is it too something that has got free of its boundaries in my mind?).

The scattered dark shapes of cattle interrupt the plains. From this distance they could be anything—zebras, lions, camels. Lions escaped once, not so far from here, from a travelling carnival, and in the days before their recapture sightings and tracks were reported everywhere. There is a ripple along the line of the horizon, a band of mirage which separates land from sky. As I drive it shifts and changes. Magic water, we called it when we were children. Somewhere behind its reflection the travellers keep pace with me.

We are passing through a place described on the maps as lion country. I think it is so-called in order to give a name to the forces which inhabit this place. They are not lions, of that I am sure. I think they are the demons we carry about in our own minds, loosed by something in this place, so that each of us is beset by our own secret terror. Only the child and Chance seem unaffected. I can only hope we have gone beyond this region of chimaera before the expedition loses its resolve.

The mapmaker's tale radiates across the landscape. It is a glancing narrative, its structure spatial rather than continuous. Along one of its trajectories a mysterious stranger rides towards the point of departure. Along another, two border women bring a child they have discovered in the desert. The man and the child must arrive to complete the imperative for the new journey. The people are restless. Children gather to throw stones at the mapmaker, and leave to seek their own unmapped places. A band of horsemen, bathed in icy light, ride out in pursuit of shadows and return from some bloodstained encounter. On the periphery of each event squat the mud men, watching.

These travellers have been with me a long time. I know that they have set out to retrace an ancient seasonal route, recorded in their songs from a time before the lakes of their homeland dried up. I know the mapmaker's uneasy knowledge in some way complements my own, and that she must make the final stages of the journey alone. The travellers' tale has an inner logic that intercepts mine, but I do not examine it too closely. Although they pass from time to time through the grooved contours of my mind, their pilgrimage is independent of mine.

The first sand dunes become visible on the horizon, and I leave the lion country behind.

25

I CAMP AT THE FOOT OF A low sandstone escarpment to the south-east of Pedestal Hills, a belt of dead gidgee giving me the best campfire I've had for the whole trip. Every time I make camp I'm aware of the legacy I have inherited. The way I make camp is the way my father did it, the way I carry the axe and walk out across the water-washed flat to the belt of low dead trees. The way I am here, in this country. The way I lay the fire. How old was I when he taught me these things? The billy balanced on a couple of good-sized sticks to let the flames get under it. The coals lifted out of the fire, beautiful gidgee coals, laid in a pile between a couple of small logs, the camp oven resting on them. The way I move about the camp, stoke the fire, check the billy.

I wonder when humans domesticated fire. When I look into the flames of my campfire, here in the desert, my adult self remembers the campfires of my childhood, and with the memory of campfires comes the memory of voices, talk and stories which move across time and fill the darkness of my solitude. And there is always the other campfire, a little distant from the one at which I sit, and the stories and the laughter cross the space between us in a language I don't understand. And behind those memories is something more primitive than memory, a flame that illuminates a cave wall, that holds off not imagined but real danger, a darkness that is not benign like this darkness which surrounds me now.

The gidgee fire has made me very cheerful, which makes Sam happy. He lopes after me and hooks a paw around my leg, trying to trip me up. This is a favourite trick, which he used to try out on passing joggers when we went to the beach. I would deny that I had anything to do with the battled-scarred, cauliflower-eared, toothless, stone-deaf animal which seemed to claim an acquaintance with me. I shadow-box him and he grabs at my arm with his gummy jaws, and barks and barks gleefully. This good-tempered, bad-mannered dog has been a point of reference for me on this trip. No-one can have a dog like Sam and take themselves entirely seriously.

While the billy boils I set my Walkman on the bonnet of the Suzuki, plug in the tiny portable speakers and play Aaron Neville. His voice spills into the night like indigo silk, to match the colour of the sky. I climb to the top of the sandstone escarpment and dance along the edge. The last red ember on the western horizon goes out, and the soul music weaves with the smoke from the fire. I yell at the top of my voice. Tonight I will vanquish the melancholy, because for my companions I have a gidgee fire and a foolish dog and the voice of a man whose singing distills and transforms that melancholy into an invocation of beauty and faith. The night sky is a magic carpet which seems blue black, but as I look deeper and deeper I see that there are no spaces without stars. The deeper I look the more I see nothing but stars. In fact I am looking at a carpet made of light, which looks like darkness.

On the edge of the low cliff I stand and address the stars. This is the biggest audience I am ever likely to have, and I am not going to waste it. I tell them why I am here. I explain about the trip.

My father died, you see, and I had a dream. In the dream I carried my father's body on my back, searching for the right place to put it down. He was frail, but even so I had difficulty carrying him. I stumbled and struggled along the slope of a hillside. His limbs flopped and dragged, and I was angry with him that he had not taken better care of himself. I laid him down for a while in order to rest. The countryside rolled away in all directions, a place I had never seen before. I considered leaving him there on the side of that strange hillside. The look on his face was tired and a little sad. After a while I lifted the body onto my back again and kept on searching.

They say fathers invent daughters, and daughters invent fathers. The father I invented held my life in thrall for years. I felt as if my first loyalty must always be to him. I chose lovers I could leave, so I would not be faced with choices too difficult to make. I'm here alone like this because my father taught me that important things must be done alone. I believed that to need other people was a weakness. He made me believe that really important experiences could never be shared. Other people couldn't be trusted to understand, they only devalued the precious moment. I remember how special it made me feel, being the only one who was exempt. Later I drew back from this favoured position, but something of it always flavoured the relationship between us. I felt a great responsibility towards my father's idea of me. I knew how far short of it I fell, but I could not bear it that he might see how foolish and cowardly I really was. I invented myself for him again and again, until I did not know how to be anyone else.

He died, and I grieved for him intensely, but I did not want him to be alive again. He had to die before I could begin to escape his idea of me. But I know as well that his belief in me is what lets me do things like this, to take off into the desert on a lone pilgrimage, to choose to be an artist, to determine to live life on my own terms. In the very act of trying to free myself from him, I am aware that he made it possible for me to do the things necessary to free myself.

—Help me! I say to the stars.—Help me to put his body down.

Their light is cold and limitless. They don't encourage me in this folly of patricide. I feel self-conscious and a little foolish.

Sam has gone away down to the camp and the fire, where he waits pensively for his dinner. This is a dog's life, going hungry while his person is up there on the hill talking to the stars. She doesn't do this sort of thing very often, though he knows better than anyone the brunt of her rare rages. Such is the purpose of dogs.

I stand for a while, looking out towards the silhouettes of the Pedestal Hills. In the darkness they are low blunt shapes against the horizon. They are presences, not threatening but impassive, distinctly alive. I wonder what ancestral drama created them, what beasts crouch inside their sandstone skin. I am struck that so few people have stood here, that this is one of the least populated places on the earth. Davidson approached with his camels from the north-west, naming the country as he came. He did not see the evidence of some primordial scuffle scattered across the landscape. Instead he recognised in them the iconography of his own culture, and named them accordingly. I'm sure he didn't stand on a cliff and recount his dreams to the indifferent stars. A cool wind is coming out of the west. Soon it will drive me off my sandstone soapbox.

LIVING OUT HERE SET US APART. The mysterious glamour of isolation rubbed off on us, made us special. This country is mythological, ancestral. You can't live in it and not be touched by it. It is a curious experience to grow up in mythological country. It is possibly like being very beautiful. It is the thing people notice about you, that makes you different and unique. It becomes the way you identify yourself. This is where I come from. This is my country. This is me.

Families who live in isolated places become a world unto themselves. There is no peer group to dissipate loyalties, no role models beyond the immediate circle to suggest that there are other ways in which to interpret the world. Neighbours, hundreds of kilometres away and seen rarely, are the same in kind as one's own family, sometimes more so. We are small tribes, passionate defenders of our particular identity.

There was nothing adversarial in our relationship to this place. Even in the worst stretches of heat-stricken, windless January, when we did nothing but drag the pump-jack from bore to bore in a desperate bid to keep the water up to the perishing stock, we were never against the country. It was home, and we loved it because we had made it ours and because we had consented to the claim it made on us. All the family felt this in different ways. My brothers and sister took it for granted. They left their bare footprints daily in the red earth and did not question the rightness of their belonging to this place. I did not have this certainty, feeling always that my place in it was provisional, that there was another world in which I felt both exiled and seduced. So I loved it passionately, feeling always that I must prove my love, feeling always on the brink of betraying it. This has not changed.

The thing I hungered for, though I could not have formulated it, was the articulation of an interior voice. I knew such a language was possible, for I found it in the books I read. Subtle and suggestive, oblique and revealing, it gave substance to the things which I knew scratched and left their marks beneath the visible surfaces of life. The language of my world was anecdotal, practical, concrete. At its best, in its dark laconic humour, it acknowledged the unsayable. But more often it was alcohol, or the grievances of women, that unleashed some anguished intemperate noise. It emerged misshapen and savage, attacked and did harm, and went back into hiding. No wonder people feared it.

So I burrowed into the mythologies and stories that grew out of green places in another hemisphere, and acquired an appetite my dry, ochre-coloured world could not feed.

I believed in the myth of the Outback. The solitary hero scratches his iconography of heroic failure. He tells himself into the country with stories of endurance and luck and foolhardiness. It's heady stuff. But when you start to take the myth apart, you are left with—the myth of the Outback. It is irreducible. The focus may shift a little, depending on your point of view. Its heroes at any given time may be black, or women, or both. The intrepid explorer may be reinterpreted as egocentric and incompetent, the laconic male as an insensitive buffoon, but that is barely relevant in the context of the country itself.

It seems that everyone carries around their own mythology of the Outback, or the inland—an interesting distinction, since one implies going outwards and the other inwards. A myth of extroversion or a myth of introversion. Both have become deeply embedded in the cultural psyche of this country. Men like Davidson and my father lived the extrovert myth, of heroism and achievement and conquest. And yet my father at least was primarily compelled by the introvert myth, of the spiritual quest, the mysterious source. The extrovert myth is presently out of favour, being subjected to the scrutiny of postcolonial interpretation. The introvert myth is still intact, but is becoming progressively confused and conflated with the Aboriginal attachment to land. White Australians are becoming disenfranchised from any right to a deep sense of connection to country, the impulse towards the sacred which has always driven human beings to establish a sense of meaning and belonging.

It seems to me that the difference between white and Aboriginal myths of country is that Aborigines rarely seek solitude in the landscape. For the most part they are thoroughly frightened by the notion of being alone in it. They have an infrastructure of beliefs and stories and prohibitions which weave them into the country, so that they are as enmeshed in it as they are enmeshed in family, so that they have obligations to it that are as powerful and of the same nature as the obligations to family. The distinction between the practical and the spiritual is not delineated. It is all part of the same thing.

The most compelling of the whitefellow myths is the myth of solitude. It is about finding some sort of redemption in the solitary encounter with a spiritual domain, which is epitomised by the desert. There is an element of gnosticism in this, the notion of the direct encounter with the spiritual source, the heretic and outsider who chooses to meet god alone in the wilderness.

The magical darkness that is made of light has taken my words away and turned them into stars. They glimmer back at me, stripped of meaning. The gidgee fire is burning low.

DEATH GIVES LIFE A PECULIAR clarity. It is as if another dimension opens suddenly into the world. When the death is in your own family, you feel it in the cells of your body, a kind of genetic shudder that recognises the extinguishment of some of its own material. It was as if during those first stages of grief I understood something essential of the poised fragile balance of life. There were other things too, which had no place or name in our sophisticated death-denying society.

After the accident I went to see the pilot of the smashed helicopter. He survived, with a damaged spine and shattered legs. Partly I knew I had to see him for his sake, but it wasn't for his good I went, it was for my own. I had to see the man who had killed my father. I sat by his hospital bed, said all the right things, absolved him of blame, and all the while I could feel forces circling like vultures, just waiting for the moment to flap in, relentless and ugly, and pick out the eyes first, and the tongue, and the genitals, soft as a flower.

I wanted to consume this damaged body and make it part of myself. Poor man, it's just as well he never knew. He had enough on his plate, with the terrible pain, the wondering if he would walk again, the agony of responsibility for the death of a man. I watched myself, neat and contained, at the centre of these circling things. They had a look of something very old, familiars come to carry out their proper function among the rites of death and grieving. They hulked behind the conventions of good-mannered grief. When I walked along the hospital corridors I felt them flop and scurry behind me, though when I turned to look there was nothing but green linoleum tiles and the late winter light of the tropics falling through tall windows. It was only indoors that they oppressed me, where their harsh archaic substance encountered polished resistant surfaces, plastic and metal, or the tidy shapes of constraint. When I stood among the box gum and quinine and ironbark, shadows moved like the shadows of leaves and birds, and an ancient gaze followed me from the grooves of creased bark. When I stood in the forest and howled, something settled softly around me and carried my grief away into the corners of the forest, so that this tree might contain some of it, and that pile of leaves, and the reddish squat mounds of anthills.

Now, as I look out across the star-illumined landscape, I see the shapes of grief, settled and quiet, in the crouching hummocks of the Pedestal Hills. Hold it for me, I tell them quietly, hold it for me here in this place which he loved.

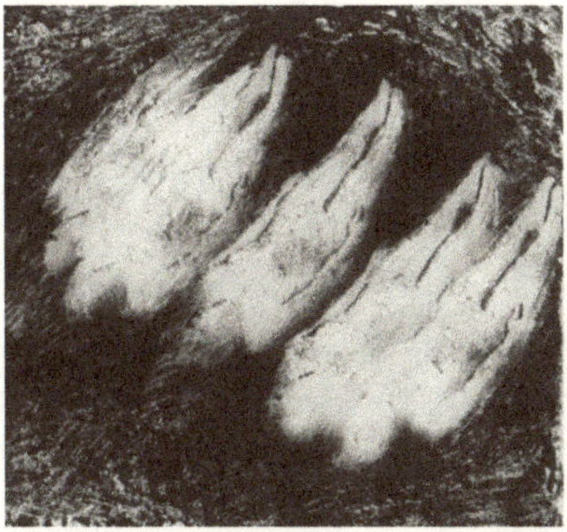

26

THE FENCE LINES, THE NEW TANKS, the stubble plains are a transparent screen across my mind's eye, through which I can still make out the contours of the old country. Between the screen that is the present and the memory that is the past lie the twenty years in which my family went away, reluctantly, out of necessity, and made another part of the country home. It is to that place we all return now, touching base from time to time, that country which holds a seam of shared memory longer and deeper than this one. My mother has re-established her life there, in the place where my father died. Grandchildren have been born for whom it is the family centre, the magic country of adventure. But it is here, where I am now, that continues to be the myth country.

Myth emerges out of some conjunction of landscape and the human mind. Put us together, people and place, and myth is inevitable. If the place is violent and alienating, then so is the myth. Urban myths are of a different order than pastoral myths. With the pastoral myth goes the notion of harmony, balance, spiritual sustenance, a lost Edenic past. The remnant aboriginal cultures scattered about the world exercise a sentimental grip on the contemporary imagination, and it is not surprising. An old Aboriginal woman, watching a pelican flying low over water, said—That Tjama's nephew, and then told a dreamtime story of the pelican. The bird continued its slow elegant flight, ancestor and dead boy and bird together winging across blue water, and I had the smallest glimpse, gone as quickly as it had been apprehended, of how it all worked.

How do I pick my way through the densely woven texture of story, memory and myth? How much does memory submit to the myth, which after all is the foundation of the story? And what is the story I am trying to tell anyway?

It is in part the story of a place, and of histories intersecting in that place, shaped by it and shaping it. It began with an Aboriginal story, of which I know a little, but not much. Davidson's journey opened up the Granites and Tanami goldmines. My father's journey established a stock route and a cattle station. My own journey affects nothing but my own life. Is this because I am a woman, or because of the time I live in, or both? It might be different, should I choose to stay. But I won't. I belong to an age whose experience is one of displacement and a kind of loss. The thing lost will continue to haunt me, and the idea of loss will be located in a particular place. The loss is part of the myth.

And what of my story? I can't tell it all, or even very much of it. Again and again the words dissolve. The myth I thought I had come back to lay weaves around me with its own particular logic. When I sit in the dirt beside Margaret and talk with her she says—You were born in this country, you Napurrula and this country here is your country.

I was not born here, but the story expands to accommodate me. In a place where belonging to country is a given, where it is incomprehensible that one can survive without belonging to country, the social structure is flexible and generous. With it goes the assumption of responsibility to that country, that you will remember it and care for it. Many people, including those who are not Australian, are powerfully struck by the ancestral nature of the Australian landscape. I wonder if it is because the country has been held in the consciousness of its people in this particular way, this extraordinary identification of people with country so that the two are not distinguishable from each other. Or is it in the nature of certain places to assert a grip on the imagination of all who set foot in it, and to draw out of them whatever they have to offer?

What have I found, in this return to my father's country? As I track him he disappears, and I glimpse him instead squatting in the dappled light of the box-gum forest in Central Queensland. I thought I had come back to re-examine his story, even to challenge it, but I find instead that I am willing to let it stand. It no longer seems burdened under a weight of contradictions.

As I travel through the country I discover that this is not my country, nor is it my father's country. But my track, my story travels through it and so does his. They make up part of the pattern of the country. By coming back I reinvoke them. At all the points of intersection I feel the other journeys, ancestral, contemporary, historic, imaginary. They are all under my skin.

27

I AM AWARE THAT THIS JOURNEY at least is almost over. I want to be gone. For the time being I have used up my small quota of courage. I no longer know what this country means to me, whether I can bear to come back.

I make my last camp at Lake Ruth. At the homestead store there is a brief meeting with the Tanami Aboriginal women, a little awkward. Later they come to the camp for a visit. I hunt out as many cups and mugs as I can find and make a billy of tea. The women spoon in sugar, not too much, laughing, telling me they are all supposed to lose weight. We sit together in the afternoon shade of the ti-tree, and Patricia points out a solitary desert gum on the northern edge of the lake. She tells me it is an old man, one of the ancestors, who healed a group of dreamtime warriors with red ochre after they were burned in a bushfire near the present site of the homestead. In good seasons people camped here, swam and hunted and made tools, dug for sand frogs near the place where I have made my camp. Margaret says that Bullock's Head Lake is called Windiki, the place of the white heron dreaming. It seems a good place to have left a man's ashes, guarded by the graceful bent-necked bird. The women ask me if I get scared, camping on my own, and I tell them not usually. Then I tell them about the night I sat in the boat and the dog got scared, and me too, when I felt the presences all about me. They nod their heads and murmur to each other, unsurprised. This is a place where the spirits are strong.

Later we dig for sand frogs in the pale sand. There is moisture below the surface, and we begin to find frogs a metre or so down. There is nothing arbitrary in the choice of a spot to dig. Patricia points out the almost imperceptible mounds the frogs make on the surface. To an untrained eye they are virtually invisible.

—Your turn, Napurrula, the women say, and I crouch in the hole, fingers probing, encountering the soft-bodied frogs in their sandy pouches. I hand them up to Margaret, who flicks an expert thumbnail, crushing a spot above the blind-looking eyes, paralysing them. In this climate they would start to rot and stink quickly if killed outright. When the hole I am in seems to have yielded up all its frogs, we walk about among the sprawling ti-tree, searching for another likely spot.

—Over here, Napurrula, the women call. —This way, Napurrula.
Sometimes it is me they are calling, sometimes Margaret.

Dora, Margaret's mother, strokes my arm with her long hands.

—Napurrula, she says. —Daughter. Tell your mother you have lot of mothers now.

—I'll tell her, I say.

The women's voices float among the trees, laughing. A language I don't understand. My mind reaches back a long way, finds a stray word, and another. *Warlu, gnapa, kuyu*— fire, water, meat. We take our haul of sand frogs back to my campfire, and the women rake a space in the hot ashes, throw in the live frogs, cover them with coals and ash. A scorched frog that has not been properly paralysed struggles from the heaving ash, crawls blindly away from the heat. Peggy pushes it back into the coals with a stick.

—Poor thing, she says perfunctorily, a sop to my white-fellow sensibilities. Here and there a tiny arm waves, a hiss of steam as the water-filled frogs boil and pop. This is a priceless lesson in bush tucker, I tell myself. But I think I would have to kill them first.

Finally all movement in the coals ceases, the shrunken roasted bodies are scooped out and dusted free of ash. Patricia asks me if I have any salt. She picks up a frog, breaks it open, delicately picks out the small sac of frog shit. They are mere sacs of guts with leathery vestigial limbs. I know I am going to have to eat at least one. Next to me Peggy prepares a frog, hands it to me, grinning, a partly chewed corpse visible behind her broad yellow teeth. I pick tentatively around the edges of my frog, to the vast amusement of the women. The other Peggy sympathises. She doesn't like them either. *Nyilyapunta*—sand frog. I test the word and the women laugh, pleased with my accent. My tongue, trained in babyhood, remembers how to make the sounds. *Mangari*—tucker. That one I remember.

I feel curiously diminished among these women. They occupy physical space in a way I don't. This is not merely because they are mostly much larger than I am. They inhabit their bodies unapologetically. Most of them have experienced physical violence, both as recipients and perpetrators. They are mothers and grandmothers and great-grandmothers. Their bodies express a primary femaleness from which I am excluded. I am not overly burdened with vanity, but I am a product of my own culture, with its emphasis on youthfulness, its peculiarly antiseptic notions of attractiveness.

The old woman, Dora, has a look about her I recognise as characteristic of these desert women when they become very old. The shape of the skull predominates, the features stretch and simplify. The fleshiness of the younger faces is refined and reduced, until what is left is the crafted bone shell which houses knowledge I cannot begin to imagine, which may simply be knowledge of how to continue to survive.

Margaret would be remarkable anywhere. She is so tall, a shy and gentle matriarch. She is clearly the central strength of this extended family, a woman whose natural dignity makes one draw with genuine humility on the best in oneself. Her skull is recently scarred at the hairline, a shiny bald patch evidence of self-wounding sorry business. My shyness collides with hers, we struggle to cross the barrier of language. Margaret speaks five languages, but English is the least of them. We are both relieved when Patricia takes up the thread. Patricia is clever, literate, her English excellent. She has a dry edge entirely lacking in Margaret. It is this edge which allows her to negotiate the whitefellow world successfully. She does not have her mother's extraordinary dignity, but is formidable in her own way. Beverly is a child on the edge of adolescence, her inheritance the lineage of power and knowledge passed down through these women. She belongs to the generation which will inherit the new century.

In spite of the troubled questions raised by land rights, the politics of dispossession, which now crosses racial boundaries, I feel optimistic among these women. Sitting with them, I feel my own ambivalence settle. I know this is temporary, but for a time we all occupy the same sunlit, shade-dappled, woodsmoke fragrant afternoon.

A SMALL WIND WHISPERS IN the ti-tree. The afternoon light falls on the blue water of the lake. Across the fire from me the other woman sits, her shirt and jeans the same blue as the water. Her body has something of the same quality as the Aboriginal women, in spite of her sunburned leanness. It is stretched, scarred, burned, loosened. It has a sense of itself which is linked directly to the proud girl who faced a man across firelight and did not relent. It is the body which animates the ochre imprints on my groundsheet, which says I am not ashamed to inhabit myself, I am not ashamed of my own anarchy, I am not afraid of the scent on my skin, which is not contamination but simply the smell of being alive.

You see, her voice says inside my head, *this is what I have*.

The voices of children come faintly from the water's edge, their small dancing figures framed in arcs of spray. From this distance it is impossible to tell whether they are black or white. Do I imagine my sister's blonde plaits on one of them, my youngest brother's gingery thatch? An old man, tree-shaped, watches from the northern shore, the burned warriors lie recuperating in the shade nearby. The people are walking in from the north, small family groups, coming down along the track from Tanami. As they reach the water's edge they laugh and throw down their bundles, and fling themselves into the water. The black stockmen practise high jumping, and let my father win the footraces at the Christmas Eve picnic. My mother watches, suppressing a moment of quiet revolt. The women track a python to its nest in a rabbit burrow, and kill it with a long-handled shovel. I dance with the horsebreaker to the thin wail of Slim Dusty records played on an old battery-operated machine. Later I wade to the eastern shore, the country of the Tanamites, and let my childhood go.

The women have all gone now.

—Goodbye, goodbye. See you next time, Napurrula, they say. —You can come back any time.

The one in blue is the last to leave. *Come back any time*, she says. *I'll be here.*

28

THE MORNING IS STILL AND CLEAR. The boat remains where I abandoned it, halfway across the lake bed. Sam tracks me as I walk out and overturn it, then sit cross-legged on its curved base. It is so quiet. Now, in the silence, something longer than memory reaches out and clears my mind. I came back because I could not stay away. Monkarrurpa, this old, still place, holds me like a cupped palm.

On a tall anthill near a dry lake a child stands watch. Her gaze is directed toward the sand-ridge country to the south, from where she believes the mapmaker must return. After a time she retreats from her lookout to the camp, where makeshift shelters have been erected, for the days are becoming hotter. From one of these she collects the mapmaker's leather satchel and carries it to the edge of the claypan. The child takes the objects from the satchel and lays them out carefully on the dry surface. In a pouch she finds a cylinder of soft leather. Unrolled, it proves to be a map. She examines it for a time, her fingers tracing the contours and landmarks it describes. Selecting a tapering polished bone from the mapmaker's tools, the child walks out onto the lake and begins tentatively to scratch marks on its crumbling surface.

Travelling away from this country I cannot believe I am really leaving. For hours the road unreels behind me like Ariadne's thread. For hours I drive feeling the impulse to turn around and follow it back. Somewhere along the track I divest myself of Napurrula. She can stay behind, where she belongs. One day, if I can face the dilemmas and contradictions she poses, I will come back. I feel a kind of tearing, something too deep to call grief. I have raised old ghosts, rather than laid them. They have put on new skins and come up out of the earth to haunt me. By coming back I have begun something which I do not yet understand. Everywhere I have travelled I have seen my father's tracks. My footprints have overlaid his, but they have not obliterated them. I have stood alone in the places where he stood alone, and felt strange, dangerous things. But they are not the things he felt. I do not know what it was that he felt, in the days and months and years that he was in this place. Such things can't be shared. I have glimpses, intimations, but that is all. I do not know what sense he made of it. Was there time, in the spinning moment before the helicopter smashed into the ground, to make sense of anything? My own life rises out of the moment of impact and surrounds me like an exhaled breath. The next breath, the inhalation, is my own. The puzzle of fragments I have tried to reassemble frames the shape of absence. The conversation with my father is finished, and I have had the last word. There is no sense of victory. Only an emptiness, a lacuna in the soul, sucking into itself the scraps and fragments of a human life. Mine or his? It doesn't matter.

Acknowledgements

IN THE YEARS I HAVE SPENT working on this manuscript I have been fortunate in the help, encouragement and support of many people. Most of it was written while living on a small farm owned by my friends Sally Lee and Geoffrey Simpson, providing me with a place from which to retreat from the more insistent demands of daily life. At a point when I no longer knew whether the manuscript contained anything of interest to others, I showed it to Martin Harrison, whose enthusiasm persuaded me to continue, and who provided me with ongoing and invaluable editiorial advice. I was fortunate too in the support of Barbara Blackman, whose encouragement and practical help assisted me over the first hurdle towards publication. Thanks should also go to Mary Cunnane who brought a clear and professional eye to the later stages of the manuscript. From Julia Stiles I learned about good editing, and am forever humble before it. Thanks to Dr Julie Marcus for permission to quote from the letters of Olive Pink, and to Heather Curdie for her professional commitment to the book. Hamish Sewell saw the reverse side of the writing process, and Pam Lofts knows more of the inside story than most. To all these people I offer my gratitude and thanks.